THE COLLECTION OF STUFFED DOLLS
FROM A FANCY WORLD

BY KYOKO YONEYAMA

CONTENTS

Published by Ondorisha Publishers, Ltd.
32 Nishigoken-cho, Shinjuku-ku, Tokyo, Japan

Copyright©1976 by Ondorisha Publishers, Ltd.
All Rights Reserved

ISBN 0-87040-401-6

Printed in Japan

FROM FAIRY TALES
Alice in a Wonderland

INSTRUCTIONS ON PAGE 67

Carlen in Red Shoes

INSTRUCTIONS ON PAGE 72

A Red Hood

INSTRUCTIONS ON PAGE 69 ❸

MARY

CARRY

ROLA

JOE   BESS

Women

MEG

EMY

INSTRUCTIONS ON PAGE 80

7

Monday's child is fair of face,
Tuesday's child is full of grace,
Wednesday's child is full of woe,
Thursday's child has far to go,
Friday's child is loving and giving,
Saturday's child works hard for his living,
And the child that is born on the Sabbath day
is bonny and blithe, and good and gay.

Monday's child

Tuesday's child

Wednesday's child

Thursday's child   Friday's child   Saturday's child   Sabbath day's child

The Sound of Music
MARIA

My Fair Lady
ELLAIZA

INSTRUCTIONS ON PAGE 90

HUG-DOLLS

Rozaly

INSTRUCTIONS ON PAGE 93

• Elenne •

INSTRUCTIONS ON PAGE 94 ⓭

Mayu

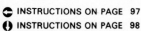
● INSTRUCTIONS ON PAGE 97
● INSTRUCTIONS ON PAGE 98

Shigeru & Chiko

17

Midori & Oyuki

INSTRUCTIONS ON PAGE 104

19

INSTRUCTIONS ON PAGE 106

Lilliputians in Woods

INSTRUCTIONS ON PAGE 109

Stray Angels

Fantasy

INSTRUCTIONS ON PAGE 112 ㉕

The Land of Pre-Birth-Babies

Nymph Ondeena

INSTRUCTIONS ON PAGE 114

INSTRUCTIONS ON PAGE 116

29

Pippi
with Long Stockings

INSTRUCTIONS ON PAGE 118

Gypsy Mam
a Fortune-Teller

INSTRUCTIONS ON PAGE 121

A Witch Under the New Moon

INSTRUCTIONS ON PAGE 125

INSTRUCTIONS ON PAGE 127

At Home on a Rainy Day

INSTRUCTIONS ON PAGE 130

INSTRUCTIONS ON PAGE 136

INSTRUCTIONS ON PAGE 138

John & Bahballa

INSTRUCTIONS ON PAGE 140

Mimi & Rulu & Popo

Princess from Bamboo

INSTRUCTIONS ON PAGE 1

夕やけ小やけ

Glowing Sunset

INSTRUCTIONS ON PAGE 145

MARIONETTS

Mitch, the Hanging Doll

INSTRUCTIONS ON PAGE 146

Rommy & Dron

INSTRUCTIONS ON PAGE 148

Sharlly

INSTRUCTIONS ON PAGE 152

GENERAL INFORMATION FOR A STUFFED DOLLS

LET'S MAKE "HIJI"

Hiji is a placid hug-doll featured by the big oval head. The course of doll-making is shown step by step on the following page. If you are just a beginner, try to learn those following basic manners before you try on another doll. You will know the skillfull manners in making much faster. The size of head is much dependent upon your make. It may become bigger, it may become smaller, but when you sew on hairs you should take care not to make any clear spots on it.

FINISHED SIZE: 37 cm tall

The key point to make a good doll is to learn the basic manners of how to form a doll-foundation, especially the work of stuffing, which may give a fine look to the finished work. Dolls are also featured by the color of hairs, the sort of clothes to be put on, and also the balance of those made on the doll makes its looks.

You may not able to get all the materials stated here, so try to make use of the things around you. If you are troubled about the combination of colors on her, use the materials of some color various in shades.

HOW TO MAKE "HIJI"

★ MATERIALS:

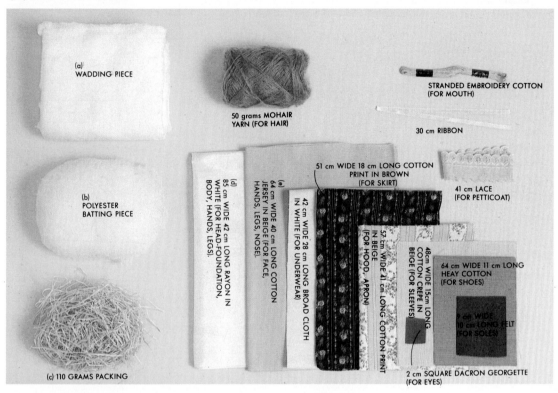

(a) WADDING PIECE

50 grams MOHAIR YARN (FOR HAIR)

STRANDED EMBROIDERY COTTON (FOR MOUTH)

30 cm RIBBON

(b) POLYESTER BATTING PIECE

(d) 85 cm WIDE 42 cm LONG RAYON IN WHITE (FOR HEAD-FOUNDATION, BODY, HANDS, LEGS).

64 cm WIDE 40 cm LONG COTTON JERSEY IN BEIGE (FOR FACE, HANDS, LEGS, NOSE).

(e) 42 cm WIDE 28 cm LONG BROAD CLOTH IN WHITE (FOR UNDERWEAR)

51 cm WIDE 18 cm LONG COTTON PRINT IN BROWN (FOR SKIRT)

41 cm LACE (FOR PETTICOAT)

57 cm WIDE 41 cm LONG COTTON PRINT IN BEIGE (FOR HOOD, APRON)

48 cm WIDE 15 cm LONG COTTON CREPE IN BEIGE (FOR SLEEVES)

64 cm WIDE 11 cm LONG HEAY COTTON (FOR SHOES)

9 cm WIDE 10 cm LONG FELT (FOR SOLES)

(c) 110 GRAMS PACKING

2 cm SQUARE DACRON GEORGETTE (FOR EYES)

(a) to (e) are required materials to make a foundation, (a) to (c) are stuffing materials to form a foundation. Prepare the stuffing materials with extra amounts. Other materials such as yarn or cotton fabrics are to be picked up from the remains you have.

Ready machine thread No. 50, 20, 8, and hand-sewing thread. When you make a foundation, use White thread with a long heavier needle.

★ TOOLS:

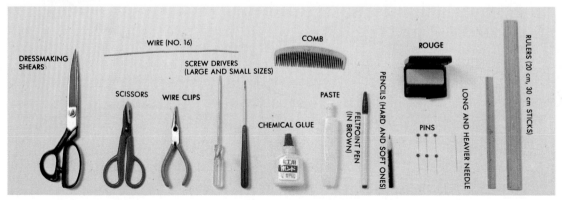

DRESSMAKING SHEARS

WIRE (NO. 16)

SCREW DRIVERS (LARGE AND SMALL SIZES)

COMB

ROUGE

RULERS (20 cm, 30 cm STICKS)

SCISSORS

WIRE CLIPS

CHEMICAL GLUE

PASTE

FELTPOINT PEN (IN BROWN)

PENCILS (HARD AND SOFT ONES)

PINS

LONG AND HEAVIER NEEDLE

1 TO MAKE PATTERNS:

Use carboard to make patterns, so that the outline of each pattern is accurately transfered on a fabric piece. Trace patterns below one by one on a piece of tracing paper and put on a cardboard piece. Transfer each pattern on to the cardboard, tracing along its outline with hard pencil. Cut all patterns out from the carboard accurately, put arrow marks which shows the grain of fabric.

GUIDE LINES BELOW:

——————— = FINISHED OUTLINE

— · — · — = OPENING FOR STUFFING

— — — — = FOLD

←———→ = GRAIN OF FABRIC LENGTH WISE

PATTERNS (ACTUAL SIZE):

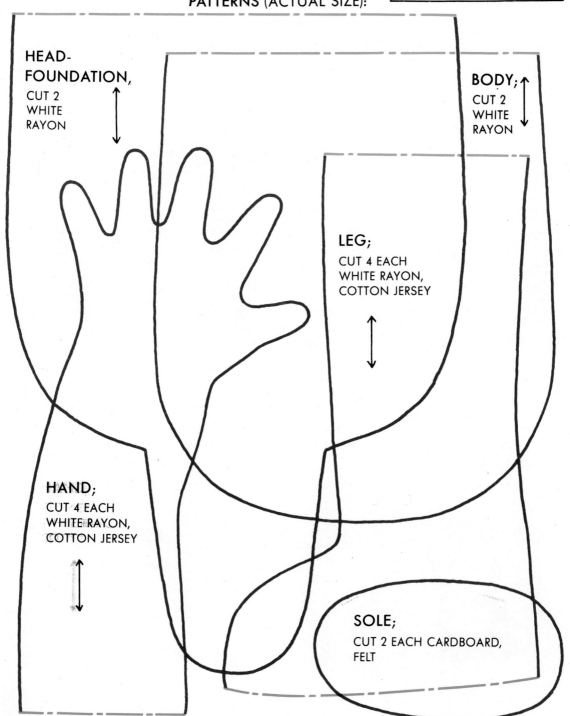

HEAD-FOUNDATION,
CUT 2
WHITE
RAYON

BODY;
CUT 2
WHITE
RAYON

LEG;
CUT 4 EACH
WHITE RAYON,
COTTON JERSEY

HAND;
CUT 4 EACH
WHITE RAYON,
COTTON JERSEY

SOLE;
CUT 2 EACH CARDBOARD,
FELT

2 TO SEW HEAD-FOUNDATION, BODY, HAND & LEGS:

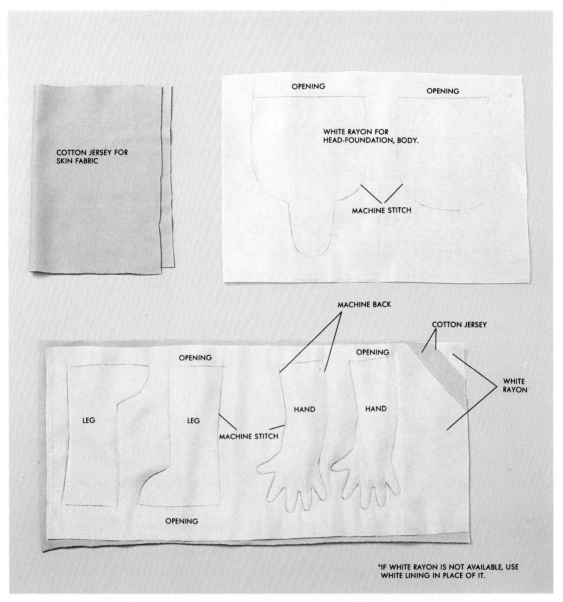

COTTON JERSEY FOR
SKIN FABRIC

OPENING   OPENING

WHITE RAYON FOR
HEAD-FOUNDATION, BODY.

MACHINE STITCH

MACHINE BACK

COTTON JERSEY

OPENING   OPENING

WHITE
RAYON

LEG   LEG   HAND   HAND

MACHINE STITCH

OPENING

*IF WHITE RAYON IS NOT AVAILABLE, USE
WHITE LINING IN PLACE OF IT.

Smooth fabric pieces with iron. Place patterns on the White Rayon with the
grain of fabric parallel to the arrowed lines on the pattern pieces. Trace patterns straightly onto the fabric with a soft pointed pencil.
Place 2 pieces of cotton jersey right sides facing between the pieces of White
rayon for hands and legs, pin the middle and around the patterns to steady
all pieces together. Machine right along the traced lines, leaving the openings
for turning. Cut out each piece putting seam allowances as follows; (1.5 cm at
the openings of hands and legs, 0.2 cm along the fingers, 0.6 cm on the others,
1.5 cm all around the head-foundation and the body).

3 TO MAKE A HEAD-FOUNDATION & A BODY:

Turn White rayon foundation pieces right side out, stuff packing as firm as possible using screw driver. If more of packing is needed, add before the previous packing is completely stuffed. Thus the foundation gives a firm and smooth finish.

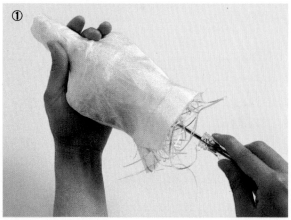

① Finish neck part of the head-foundation as firm as a bar, stuffing up to right above the opening line.

② Sew along the opening, turn its allowance to wrong side and draw to close the end firmly. Secure again, working a crossed stitch over it.

③ Stuff packing firmly into the body up to the opening. Lap up the ends, matching opening lines together and pin to steady.

④ Secure firmly with 2 strands of No. 8 machine thread, making rough stitches.

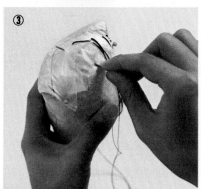

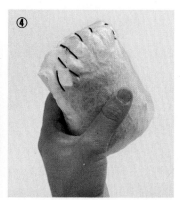

4 TO FORM THE BASE OF FACE:

From with cotton wadding tearing off into required pieces with your hand. Headfoundation, jaw, and forehead are arranged as follows.

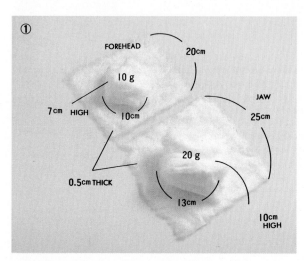

FOREHEAD
20cm
10 g
JAW
7cm HIGH
10cm
25cm
20 g
0.5cm THICK
13cm
10cm HIGH

① Make jaw and forehead respectively.

② Roll up the piece firmly, putting wadding piece for padding inside.

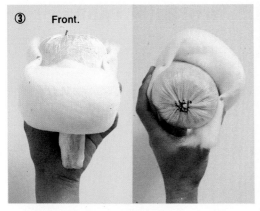

③ Front.

③ Attach jaw piece to the head-foundation with the jaw facing downward slightly, then steady with pins.

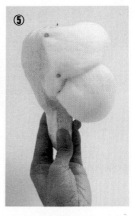

Draw the thread tightly.

④ Sew on head-foundation with No. 8 machine thread doubled, scooping largely. Tear away the surplus wadding on sides.

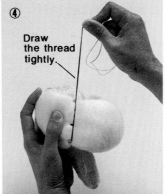

⑤ Attach forehead. Pine the piece steady, drawing lower ends on both sides slightly over to the jaw piece. Tear away the surplus of wadding, tuck in all ends.

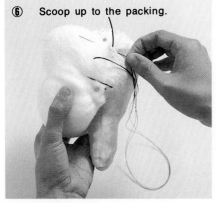

Scoop up to the packing.

⑥ Stitch the ends on side firmly to head-foundation.

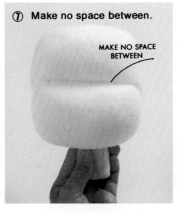

⑦ Make no space between.

MAKE NO SPACE BETWEEN

⑦ Front.

⑧ Back side.

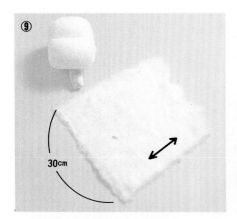

30cm

⑨ Spread wadding piece making its thickness 0.5 cm. Lay on the face biaswise.

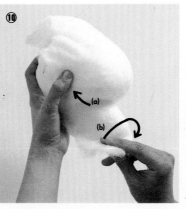

(a)

(b)

⑩ Pull wadding upward, fitting to the shape of jaw (a). Wrap the lower round the neck as (b).

⑪ Smooth surface, fitting overlaied wadding carefully to the base. Tear away the surplus on back.

5 TO COVER THE BASE OF FACE WITH SKIN FABRIC:

The skin fabric (Cotton Jersey) gives elasticity so pin the ends of stretched piece firmly to the base, then the fabric does not lossen itself.

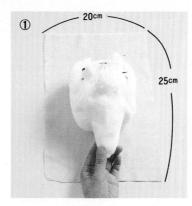

① Place face side in the middle of skin fabric.

② Pin (a) to steady. Pull up the ends on both sides at a time, making the shape of jaw clear. Pin (b) to the base secureing the fabric not to become loose.

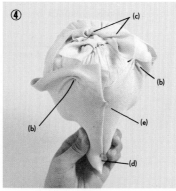

③ Twist top corners respectively, taking care not to make any folds on forehead, cross them on back and pin to steady (c).

④ Fold back the surplus center on back neck, and pin to steady (d) (e).

⑤ Stitch to the head-foundation with No. 8 machine thread doubled, pulling the fabric piece slightly upward.

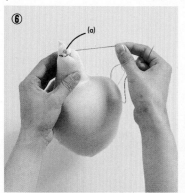

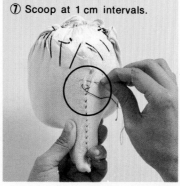

⑥ Secure (a) to the foundation, taking 3–4 stitches with single strand of No. 8 machine thread.

⑦ With the thread following, work fine stitches taking care not to make the fabric loosen at the center on back.

⑧ Finished foundation.

6 TO ATTACH EYES, NOSE & MOUTH:

Put eyes, nose and mouth on the face roughly, feature your favorite face. Put marks of their positions on the face lightly with pencil.

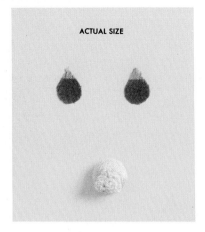

ACTUAL SIZE

TO MAKE A NOSE

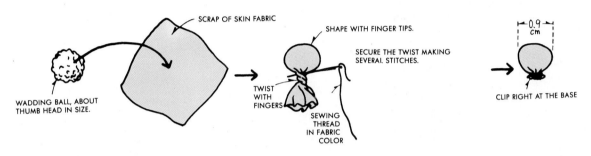

SCRAP OF SKIN FABRIC

WADDING BALL, ABOUT THUMB HEAD IN SIZE.

TWIST WITH FINGERS.

SHAPE WITH FINGER TIPS.

SECURE THE TWIST MAKING SEVERAL STITCHES.

SEWING THREAD IN FABRIC COLOR

0.9 cm

CLIP RIGHT AT THE BASE

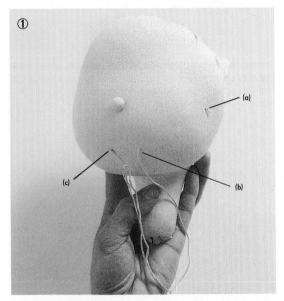

① Glue nose to position.
Use stranded cotton to make a mouth. Carry the needle through following (a) (b) (c) in turn, bring the needle out opposite to (a), fasten off the thread pulling slightly.

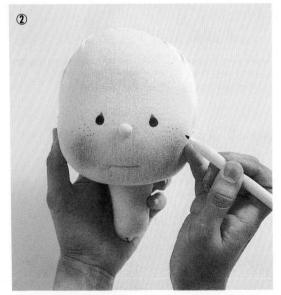

② Make eyes of dacron georgette. Draw away the threads woven crosswise to make eyelashes, cut into eye shape, glue to position.
Apply rouge using wadding piece. Put freckles lightly with felt point pen. The ink might spread on the fabric, so try on a scrap piece beforehand.

7 TO MAKE HANDS:

Make plump hands, stuffing cotton wadding into fingers, polyester batting into arms.

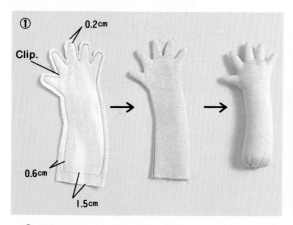

① 0.2cm
Clip.
0.6cm
1.5cm

②

③

① Cut out hands with seam allowances, clip where at the strong curve.

② Turn inside out using screw driver.

③ Turn fingers right side out one by one.

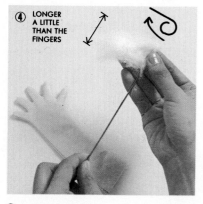
④ LONGER A LITTLE THAN THE FINGERS

⑤

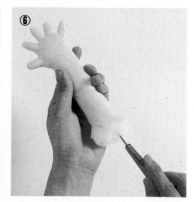
⑥

④ Wrap a piece of wadding round the wire No. 16.

⑤ Insert into each finger and pull out the wire leaving wadding piece inside.

⑥ Stuff polyester batting into hand part using screw driver. Put a little piece into palm side, making back side of the hand plump. Hand-stitch along the opening, and draw putting turning allowances inside, then fasten off.

8 TO MAKE LEGS:

Make legs stuffing cotton wadding firmly.

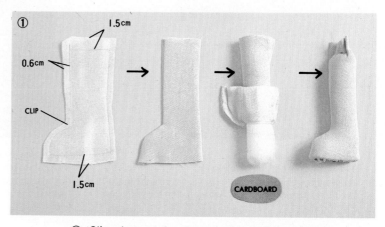

① 1.5cm
0.6cm
CLIP
1.5cm
CARDBOARD

① Clip where at the strong curve, turn the piece inside out.

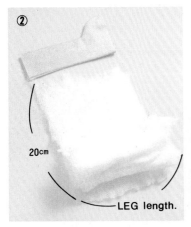

② Put a wadding piece for padding on the stretched wadding piece.

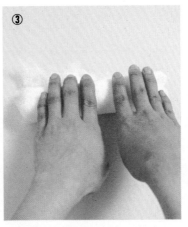

③ Roll up together with the padding inside firmly into leg size.

④ Stuff rolled up wadding into from the top opening.

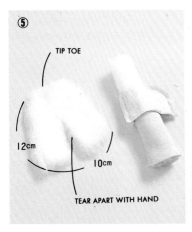

⑤ Make a stuffing piece of wadding for foot.

⑥ Put lower end of the leg between the tear, wrap with the piece following.

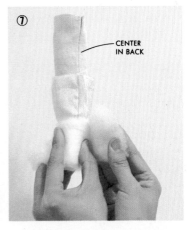

⑦ Lap up the surplus of wadding on back, pull down the foot fabric above. Stitch top opening closed and fasten off.

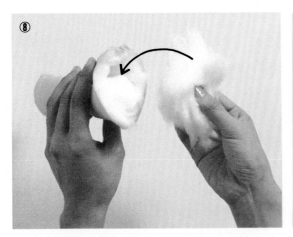

⑧ Stuff wadding up to the line of sole.

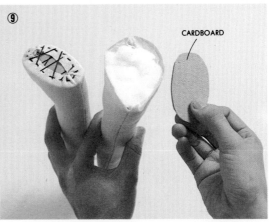

⑨ Overlay a cardboard piece. Hand-stitch along the sole and draw the thread, overcasting couple of times crosswise, then secure the end.

❾ TO PUT ON SHOES:

Cut out the pieces of shoes from fabric referring to page 62. Make using chemical glue.

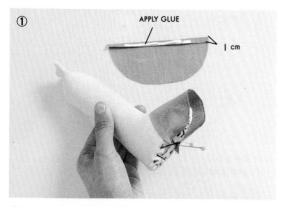

① Turn the edge of half-circle piece 1 cm to wrong side, apply glue on it. Pin to foot, covering its instep.

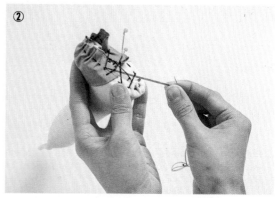

② Hand-stitch along the cut edge with No. 8 machine thread doubled, draw the thread overcasting couple of times crosswise, secure the end.

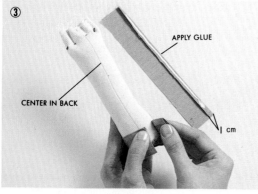

③ Turn the edge of oblong piece 1 cm to wrong side, apply glue on it. Wrap the piece round the foot, turn the end on back to wrong side, pin to steady. Finish with fine slip-stitches with the thread in fabric color.

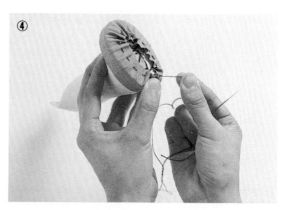

④ Hand-stitch along the edge with No. 8 machine thread doubled, draw the thread overcasting crosswise, secure the end.

⑤ Pine felt sole to the base and sew on, working fine slip-stitches.

⑥ Finished foot.

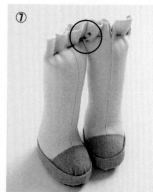

⑦ Put the finished legs together, join at the top taking a stitch to make their length equal.

10 TO SEW EACH SECTION ON THE BODY:

Check each section whether the work is correctly done, then sew on body.

① Sew legs firmly on the body front with 2 strands of No. 8 machine thread.

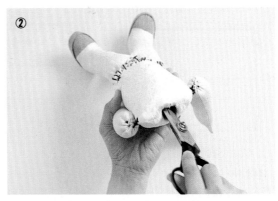

② Sew hands on the body in same manner as button-sewing. Make a cut where at the top of the body at right angles to the seam line, hole putting scissors' top into and turn to enlarge up to neck size.

③ Insert the neck into.

④ Stitch firmly (so as not the head totters) to the body, bringing the needle back through the neck in the middle to front with 2 strands of No. 8 machine thread.

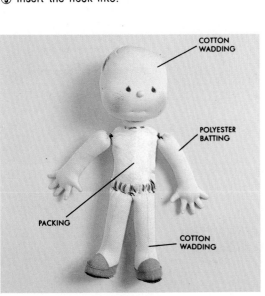

COTTON WADDING

POLYESTER BATTING

PACKING

COTTON WADDING

ABOUT STUFFING MATERIALS:

Use three types of stuffing materials, namely, Packing, Cotton Wadding, and Polyester Batting. Each material has to be used depending on the section to be made, functions or features of the doll you make.

- Packing is a lump of fine strips of wooden shavings and mainly used to form head-foundation or body of which finish has to be firm and secure.
- Ready cotton wadding as it is purchased in size. This is mainly used for face, fingers, and legs which have to be finished softly and yet firmly. If the piece is required to be cut, tear off roughly with hand instead of using scissors.
- Polyester batting is a convenient material, for this is springy and yet doesn't become buiky. Mainly used for the parts of hands and legs where wanted to be formed softly.

11 TO SEW CLOTHES:

Doll's clothes are partly sewn beforehand, and completed each germent sewing on the body one by one.

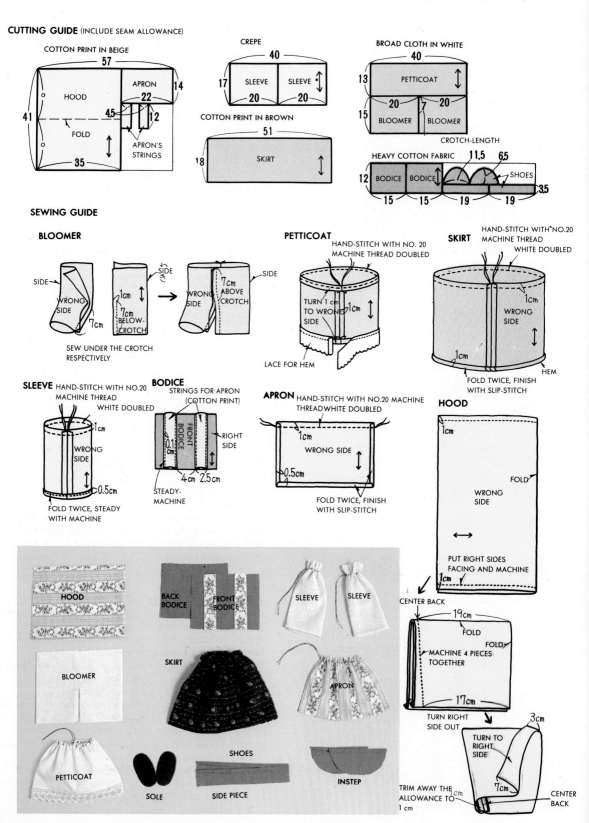

CUTTING GUIDE (INCLUDE SEAM ALLOWANCE)

COTTON PRINT IN BEIGE
- 57
- HOOD
- APRON 22 · 14
- 45 · 12
- 41 · FOLD
- APRON'S STRINGS
- 35

CREPE
- 40
- 17 SLEEVE 20 · SLEEVE 20

COTTON PRINT IN BROWN
- 51
- 18 SKIRT

BROAD CLOTH IN WHITE
- 40
- 13 PETTICOAT
- 15 · 20 · 7 · 20
- BLOOMER · BLOOMER
- CROTCH-LENGTH

HEAVY COTTON FABRIC 11.5 · 6.5
- 12 BODICE · BODICE · SHOES · 3.5
- 15 · 15 · 19 · 19

SEWING GUIDE

BLOOMER
SIDE — SIDE — SIDE
WRONG SIDE 7cm
1cm
7cm BELOW-CROTCH
WRONG SIDE
7cm ABOVE CROTCH — SIDE
SEW UNDER THE CROTCH RESPECTIVELY

PETTICOAT
HAND-STITCH WITH NO. 20 MACHINE THREAD DOUBLED
TURN 1 cm TO WRONG SIDE — 1cm
LACE FOR HEM

SKIRT
HAND-STITCH WITH NO.20 MACHINE THREAD WHITE DOUBLED
1cm
WRONG SIDE
1cm — HEM
FOLD TWICE, FINISH WITH SLIP-STITCH

SLEEVE
HAND-STITCH WITH NO.20 MACHINE THREAD WHITE DOUBLED
1cm
WRONG SIDE
0.5cm
FOLD TWICE, STEADY WITH MACHINE

BODICE
STRINGS FOR APRON (COTTON PRINT)
FRONT BODICE
0.1cm — RIGHT SIDE
4cm · 2.5cm
STEADY-MACHINE

APRON
HAND-STITCH WITH NO.20 MACHINE THREAD WHITE DOUBLED
1cm
WRONG SIDE
0.5cm
FOLD TWICE, FINISH WITH SLIP-STITCH

HOOD
1cm
WRONG SIDE — FOLD
PUT RIGHT SIDES FACING AND MACHINE
1cm
CENTER BACK
19cm — FOLD
FOLD
MACHINE 4 PIECES TOGETHER
17cm
TURN RIGHT SIDE OUT
3cm
TURN TO RIGHT SIDE
7cm
TRIM AWAY THE ALLOWANCE TO 1 cm — CENTER BACK

HOOD

BACK BODICE · FRONT BODICE

SLEEVE · SLEEVE

SKIRT

APRON

BLOOMER

PETTICOAT

SOLE · SIDE PIECE · SHOES · INSTEP

12 TO SEW ON CLOTHES:

Sew on underwear first. Conceal cut ends or seam allowances with overlapped piece. Work fine stitch neatly where to be seen from the out side.

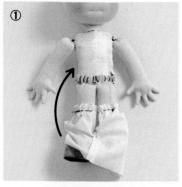

①

②

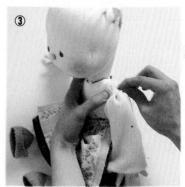

③

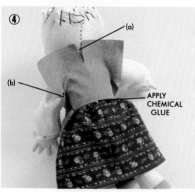

④ (a) (b) APPLY CHEMICAL GLUE

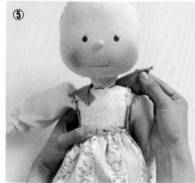

⑤

⑥

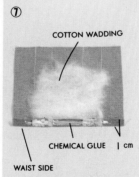

⑦ COTTON WADDING CHEMICAL GLUE | cm WAIST SIDE

⑧

⑨

① Having drawn up lower ends of the bloomers, turn the section up to waist. Tuck at four places and secure.
Put petticoat on the waist, drawing gatherings, and sew on body.

② Put skirt on the petticoat, draw gatherings setting waist slightly above the waist of petticoat, overlay apron and secure to the body.

③ Put sleeves on hands, stitch and draw at the top, secure allowances to shoulders. Gather sleeve-ends, stitching 1 cm off the edge.

④ Turn lower edge of the back bodice 1 cm to wrong side, apply chemical glue. Put it on the allowance of the skirt, pin both sides steady. Clip where at (a) & (b).

⑤ Turn the allowances of neck and arms to wrong side, pin the pieces from shoulders and sides to the body front.

⑥ Stitch to the body with 2 strands of No. 8 machine thread.

⑦ Lay wadding piece thinly over the front bodice wrong side.

⑧ Put the piece on the body front turning allowances to wrong side, secure sides and shoulders working fine slip-stitches with sewing thread.

⑨ Clothed doll.

13 TO SEW ON HAIRS AND A HOOD:

Make a bundle of yarns 160 cm long (the same length as the skein of yarn clipped at the center). Put it on the head, smoothing with the comb of coarse teeth.
Secure putting yarns following to the arrows on the chart.

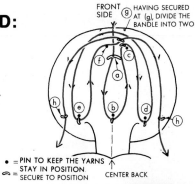

FRONT SIDE (g) HAVING SECURED AT (g), DIVIDE THE BANDLE INTO TWO

• = PIN TO KEEP THE YARNS STAY IN POSITION
‿ = SECURE TO POSITION

CENTER BACK

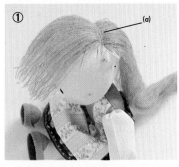

① Put front hair down on the forehead, adjusting to the width of face. Steady with the yarn carried across (a) on top slightly backward.

② Pin at the center back (b), turn the yarns up to (c).

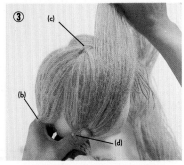

③ Pin at (c) & (d), put yarns in same manner as (2). Pass the yearn to (e), putting widely along the outline of the face.

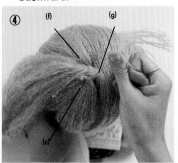

④ Having carried across the yarns up to point (g), secure each point after the (g) is secured to the head.

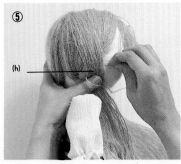

⑤ Divide the yearn left into two, put them down on both sides, secure each at (h).

⑥ Apply paste on forehead and the position of ears, attach yarns to the skin-fabric.

APPLY PASTE

⑦ Trim front hair evently. Braid the yearn on both sides, ribbon at the end.

RIBBON

⑧ Place hood on head, secure at right above the front hair and the neck back side with chemical glue.

Completed Hiji.

64

CRALLA

Shown on cover front.

The lace fabric of scalloped side is used for her dress but you may make use of colorless plain fabric together with ribbon lace.

YOU'LL NEED:
Head-Foundation, Body, Hands, Legs—90 cm by 21 cm White rayon. Face, Nose, Hands—45 cm by 25 cm Beige cotton jersey. Legs—36 cm by 21 cm White jersey. Eyes—Dacron georgette. Mouth—Stranded embroidery thread. Hair—Loop yarn. Bloomer, Petticoat—80 cm by 18 cm White broad cloth. 40 cm of 3.5 cm lace. 50 cm of 3 cm lace. Dress, Hood—15 cm by 310 cm cotton lace fabric. 50 cm of 0.6 cm ribbon. Shoes—36 cm of 1.5 cm lace. 11 cm by 5 cm felt. And Others—Packing. Cotton wadding. Polyester batting.
FINISHED SIZE: Refer to diagram.

MAKING INSTRUCTIONS:
The basic manner is same as for Hiji, so make referring to page 50–64.
Make legs under the knee in same manner as for Hiji.
Make dress and hood with lace fabric scalloped side length-wise.
Make hairs of ring winding yarn round a finger, secure each of them to the head with machine thread, taking proper space between. Secure to all the head over without clipping the yarn following.

① PATTERNS (ACTUAL SIZE):

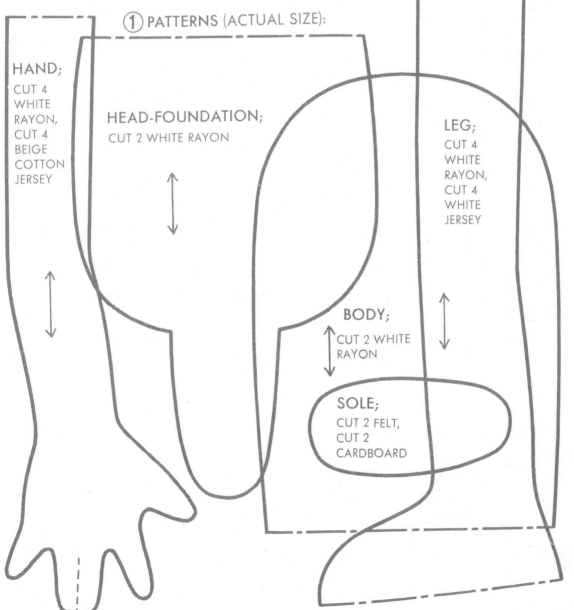

HAND;
CUT 4 WHITE RAYON, CUT 4 BEIGE COTTON JERSEY

HEAD-FOUNDATION;
CUT 2 WHITE RAYON

LEG;
CUT 4 WHITE RAYON, CUT 4 WHITE JERSEY

BODY;
CUT 2 WHITE RAYON

SOLE;
CUT 2 FELT, CUT 2 CARDBOARD

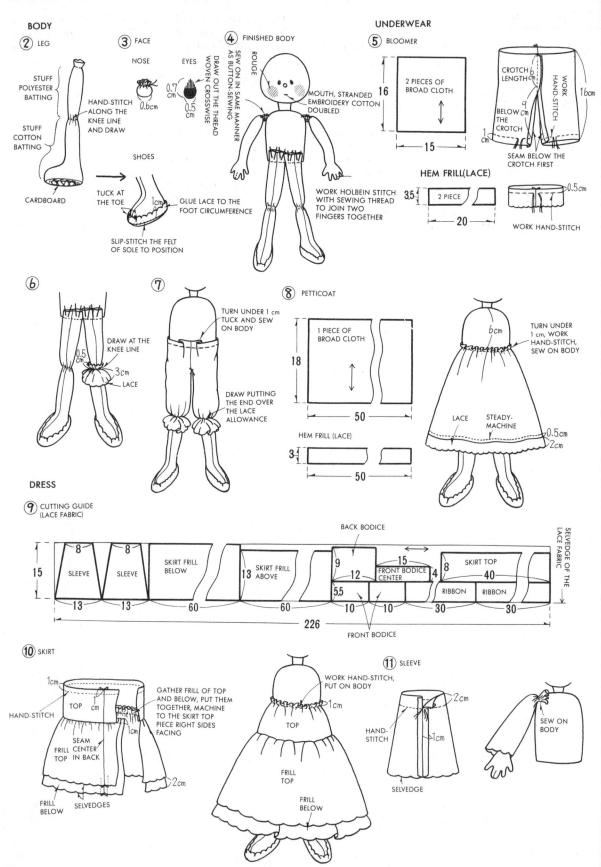

BODY

② LEG

STUFF POLYESTER BATTING

HAND-STITCH ALONG THE KNEE LINE AND DRAW

STUFF COTTON BATTING

CARDBOARD

③ FACE

NOSE

0.6cm

EYES

0.7 cm

0.5 cm

DRAW OUT THE THREAD WOVEN CROSSWISE

SHOES

TUCK AT THE TOE

1cm

GLUE LACE TO THE FOOT CIRCUMFERENCE

SLIP-STITCH THE FELT OF SOLE TO POSITION

④ FINISHED BODY

ROUGE

SEW ON IN SAME MANNER AS BUTTON-SEWING

MOUTH, STRANDED EMBROIDERY COTTON DOUBLED

WORK HOLBEIN STITCH WITH SEWING THREAD TO JOIN TWO FINGERS TOGETHER

UNDERWEAR

⑤ BLOOMER

2 PIECES OF BROAD CLOTH

16

15

CROTCH LENGTH 6 cm

WORK HAND-STITCH

16cm

BELOW THE CROTCH 9 cm

1 cm

SEAM BELOW THE CROTCH FIRST

HEM FRILL (LACE)

3.5

2 PIECE

20

0.5cm

WORK HAND-STITCH

⑥

DRAW AT THE KNEE LINE

0.5 cm

3cm

LACE

⑦

TURN UNDER 1 cm TUCK AND SEW ON BODY

DRAW PUTTING THE END OVER THE LACE ALLOWANCE

⑧ PETTICOAT

1 PIECE OF BROAD CLOTH

18

50

HEM FRILL (LACE)

3

50

6cm

TURN UNDER 1 cm, WORK HAND-STITCH, SEW ON BODY

LACE

STEADY-MACHINE

0.5cm

2cm

DRESS

⑨ CUTTING GUIDE (LACE FABRIC)

BACK BODICE

SEVEDGE OF THE LACE FABRIC

15

8

SLEEVE

8

SLEEVE

SKIRT FRILL BELOW

13

SKIRT FRILL ABOVE

9

12

5,5

FRONT BODICE CENTER

15

4

8

RIBBON

RIBBON

SKIRT TOP

40

13

13

60

60

10

10

30

30

226

FRONT BODICE

⑩ SKIRT

1cm

TOP

1 cm

HAND-STITCH

SEAM CENTER IN BACK

FRILL TOP

1cm

FRILL BELOW

SELVEDGES

2cm

GATHER FRILL OF TOP AND BELOW, PUT THEM TOGETHER, MACHINE TO THE SKIRT TOP PIECE RIGHT SIDES FACING

WORK HAND-STITCH, PUT ON BODY

1cm

TOP

FRILL TOP

FRILL BELOW

⑪ SLEEVE

2cm

HAND-STITCH

1cm

SELVEDGE

SEW ON BODY

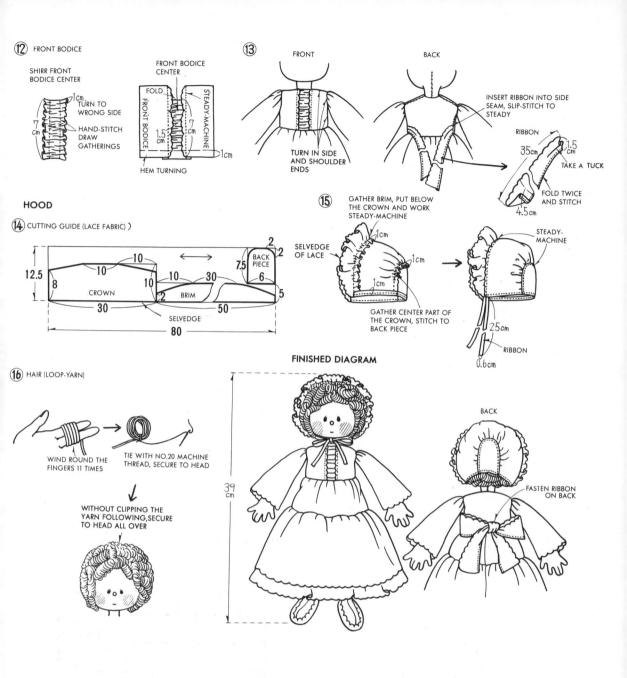

⑫ FRONT BODICE

SHIRR FRONT
BODICE CENTER

7cm
TURN TO
WRONG SIDE

7cm

HAND-STITCH
DRAW
GATHERINGS

FRONT BODICE
CENTER

FOLD FRONT BODICE

STEADY-MACHINE

1.5 cm

7 cm

1cm

HEM TURNING

⑬ FRONT   BACK

TURN IN SIDE
AND SHOULDER
ENDS

INSERT RIBBON INTO SIDE
SEAM, SLIP-STITCH TO
STEADY

RIBBON

35cm   1.5 cm

TAKE A TUCK

4.5cm

FOLD TWICE
AND STITCH

HOOD

⑭ CUTTING GUIDE (LACE FABRIC))

12.5

8

10   10

CROWN

30

10

2

10   30

BRIM

SELVEDGE

7.5   BACK PIECE

2
2

6

50

5

80

⑮ GATHER BRIM, PUT BELOW
THE CROWN AND WORK
STEADY-MACHINE

SELVEDGE
OF LACE

1cm

1cm

1cm

GATHER CENTER PART OF
THE CROWN, STITCH TO
BACK PIECE

STEADY-MACHINE

RIBBON

25cm

0.6cm

FINISHED DIAGRAM

⑯ HAIR (LOOP-YARN)

WIND ROUND THE
FINGERS 11 TIMES

TIE WITH NO.20 MACHINE
THREAD, SECURE TO HEAD

WITHOUT CLIPPING THE
YARN FOLLOWING, SECURE
TO HEAD ALL OVER

39 cm

BACK

FASTEN RIBBON
ON BACK

ALICE

Shown on page 1.

This is a hug-doll easy to make in size. Head packing should be stuffed firmly into its foundation. Mouth is drawn lightly with pencil, finished with embroidery.

YOU'LL NEED:
Head-Foundation, Body, Hands, Legs—70 cm by 35 cm White rayon. Face, Nose, Hands, Legs—50 cm by 40 cm cotton jersey. Eyes—Dacron georgette. Mouth —Stranded embroidery thread. Hair—Loop-yarn. 75 cm of 7 cm lace ribbon. Bloomer, Dress—90 cm by 40 cm cotton print. 50 cm of 3 cm lace. 280 cm of 2.5 cm lace. And Others—Packing. Cotton wadding. Polyster batting.
FINISHED SIZE: Refer to diagram.

MAKING INSTRUCTIONS:
The basic manner is same as for Hiji, so make referring to page 50–64.
Make legs stuffing polyester batting in same manner as for hands. Finish openings same way avove.
Having seamed decorative piece of front bodice and lace together, sew on body. Hand-stitch along the neck, draw and secure on back.
Sew on hair in same manner as for "A Red Hood" on page 72, trim the end evenly.

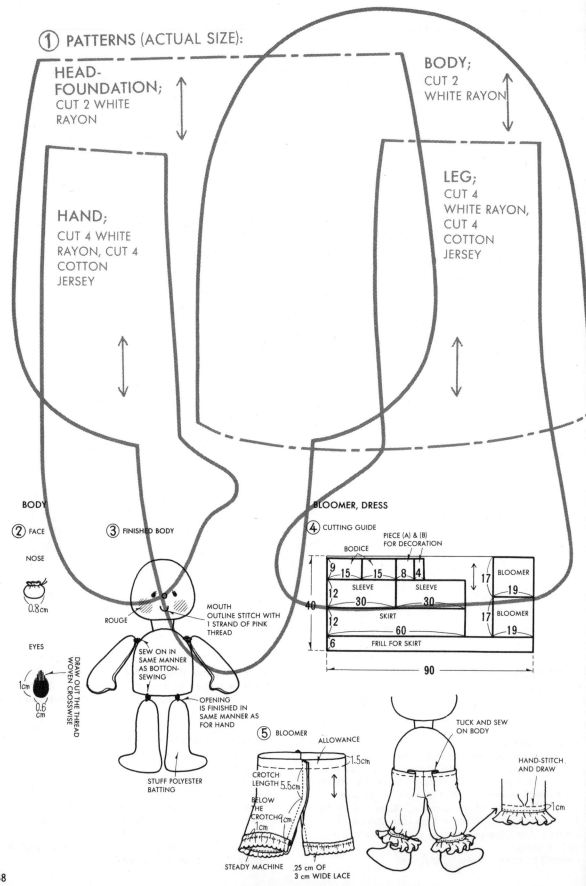

① PATTERNS (ACTUAL SIZE):

HEAD-
FOUNDATION;
CUT 2 WHITE
RAYON

BODY;
CUT 2
WHITE RAYON

HAND;
CUT 4 WHITE
RAYON, CUT 4
COTTON
JERSEY

LEG;
CUT 4
WHITE RAYON,
CUT 4
COTTON
JERSEY

BODY

② FACE

NOSE

0.8cm

ROUGE

EYES

1cm

0.6
cm

DRAW OUT THE THREAD
WOVEN CROSSWISE

③ FINISHED BODY

MOUTH
OUTLINE STITCH WITH
1 STRAND OF PINK
THREAD

SEW ON IN
SAME MANNER
AS BOTTON-
SEWING

OPENING
IS FINISHED IN
SAME MANNER AS
FOR HAND

STUFF POLYESTER
BATTING

BLOOMER, DRESS

④ CUTTING GUIDE

PIECE (A) & (B)
FOR DECORATION

BODICE

9	15	15	8	4		BLOOMER
12	SLEEVE 30		SLEEVE 30		17	19
12	SKIRT 60				17	BLOOMER 19
6	FRILL FOR SKIRT					

40

90

17

⑤ BLOOMER

ALLOWANCE
1.5cm

CROTCH
LENGTH 5.5cm

BELOW
THE
CROTCH 9cm
1cm

STEADY MACHINE

.25 cm OF
3 cm WIDE LACE

TUCK AND SEW
ON BODY

HAND-STITCH
AND DRAW

1cm

68

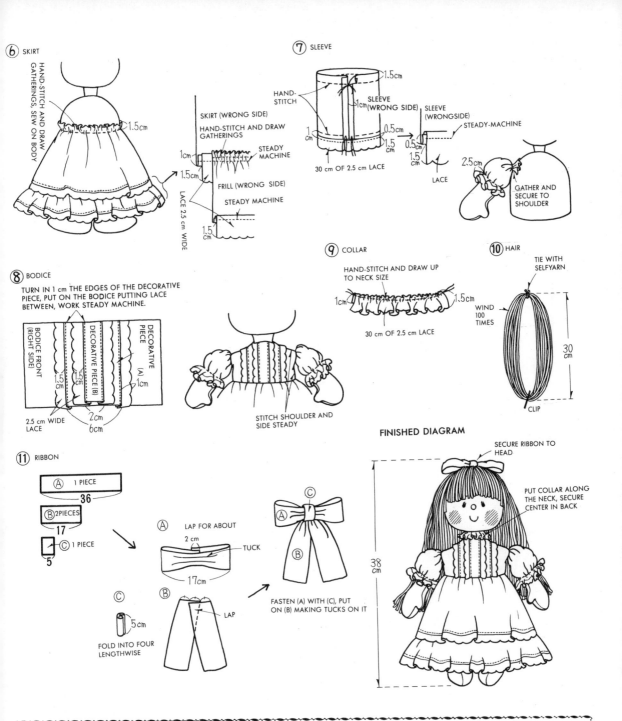

⑥ SKIRT

HAND-STITCH AND DRAW GATHERINGS, SEW ON BODY

1.5cm

SKIRT (WRONG SIDE)

HAND-STITCH AND DRAW GATHERINGS

STEADY MACHINE

1cm

1.5cm

FRILL (WRONG SIDE)

STEADY MACHINE

LACE 2.5 cm WIDE

1.5cm

⑦ SLEEVE

1.5cm

HAND-STITCH

1cm

SLEEVE (WRONG SIDE)

1cm

0.5cm

1.5cm

30 cm OF 2.5 cm LACE

0.5cm

1.5cm

SLEEVE (WRONGSIDE)

STEADY-MACHINE

LACE

2.5cm

GATHER AND SECURE TO SHOULDER

⑧ BODICE

TURN IN 1 cm THE EDGES OF THE DECORATIVE PIECE, PUT ON THE BODICE PUTTING LACE BETWEEN, WORK STEADY MACHINE.

BODICE FRONT (RIGHT SIDE)

DECORATIVE PIECE (B)

DECORATIVE PIECE (A)

1.5cm 1.5cm 1cm

2.5 cm WIDE LACE

2cm

6cm

STITCH SHOULDER AND SIDE STEADY

⑨ COLLAR

HAND-STITCH AND DRAW UP TO NECK SIZE

1cm

1.5cm

30 cm OF 2.5 cm LACE

⑩ HAIR

TIE WITH SELFYARN

WIND 100 TIMES

30 cm

CLIP

⑪ RIBBON

Ⓐ 1 PIECE
36

Ⓑ 2 PIECES
17

Ⓒ 1 PIECE
5

Ⓐ LAP FOR ABOUT
2 cm
TUCK
17cm

Ⓒ
5cm
FOLD INTO FOUR LENGTHWISE

Ⓑ
LAP

Ⓒ
Ⓐ
Ⓑ

FASTEN (A) WITH (C), PUT ON (B) MAKING TUCKS ON IT

FINISHED DIAGRAM

SECURE RIBBON TO HEAD

PUT COLLAR ALONG THE NECK, SECURE CENTER IN BACK

38 cm

A RED HOOD

Shown on page 3.

Select the materials of hood and dress in much well color. Try to finish them in different torns of color. Checked fabric of hood and apron might also make her look prettier.

YOU'LL NEED:

Head—Foundation, Body, Hands, Legs—55 cm by 52 cm White rayon. Face, Nose, Hands, Legs—65 cm by 52 cm cotton jersey. Eyes—Dacron georgette. Mouth —Stranded embroidery thread. Hair—Sport weight yarn. 40 cm of 0.3 cm ribbon. Bloomer, Petticoat—90 cm by 20 cm White broad cloth. 50 cm of 2 cm lace. Dress—82 cm by 38 cm seer-sucker. Vest—19 cm by 13 cm Pastel Orange felt. Pastel Orange stranded embroidery thread. Apron—41 cm by 100 cm seersucker. Hood—22 cm by 45 cm Vermilion felt. Shoes —20 cm by 17 cm Grey felt. Grey embroidery thread. And Others—Packing. Cotton wadding. Polyester batting.

FINISHED SIZE: Refer to diagram.

MAKING INSTRUCTIONS:
The basic manner is same as for Hiji, so make referring to page 50–64.
Make legs stuffing polyester batting in same manner as for hands. Finish openings same way as hands.

Sew on shoes made of felt beforehand.
Make hair separately, glue on head, then finish the whole.

PATTERNS (ACTUAL SIZE):

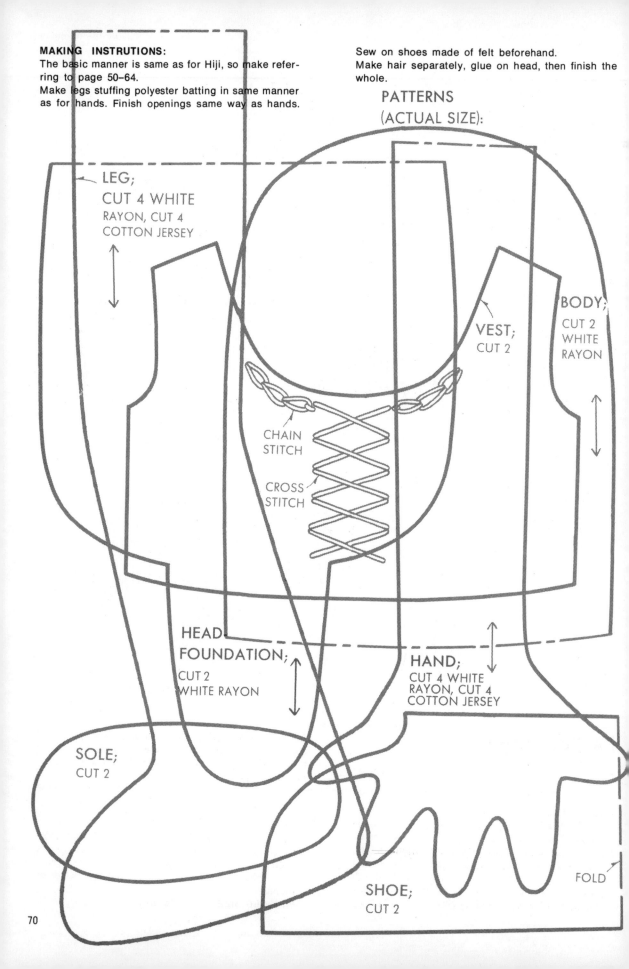

LEG;
CUT 4 WHITE
RAYON, CUT 4
COTTON JERSEY

VEST;
CUT 2

BODY;
CUT 2
WHITE
RAYON

CHAIN
STITCH

CROSS
STITCH

HEAD
FOUNDATION;
CUT 2
WHITE RAYON

HAND;
CUT 4 WHITE
RAYON, CUT 4
COTTON JERSEY

SOLE;
CUT 2

FOLD

SHOE;
CUT 2

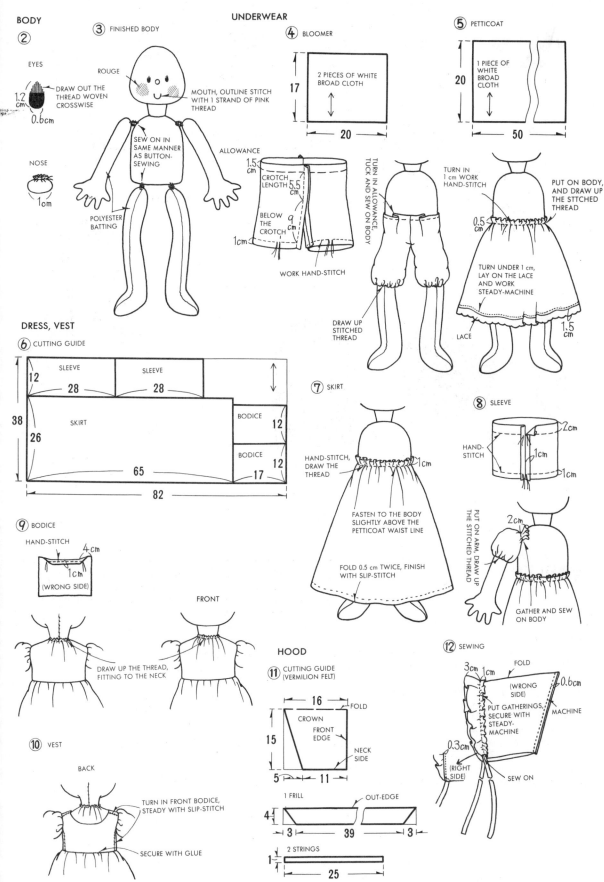

BODY

②

EYES

1.2 cm
0.6cm

DRAW OUT THE THREAD WOVEN CROSSWISE

NOSE

1cm

③ FINISHED BODY

ROUGE

MOUTH, OUTLINE STITCH WITH 1 STRAND OF PINK THREAD

SEW ON IN SAME MANNER AS BUTTON-SEWING

ALLOWANCE

POLYESTER BATTING

UNDERWEAR

④ BLOOMER

17

2 PIECES OF WHITE BROAD CLOTH

20

1.5 cm

CROTCH LENGTH 5.5 cm

BELOW THE CROTCH 9 cm

1cm

WORK HAND-STITCH

⑤ PETTICOAT

20

1 PIECE OF WHITE BROAD CLOTH

50

TURN IN ALLOWANCE, TUCK AND SEW ON BODY

TURN IN 1 cm WORK HAND-STITCH

DRAW UP STITCHED THREAD

PUT ON BODY, AND DRAW UP THE STTCHED THREAD

0.5 cm

TURN UNDER 1 cm, LAY ON THE LACE AND WORK STEADY-MACHINE

LACE

1.5 cm

DRESS, VEST

⑥ CUTTING GUIDE

12

SLEEVE 28

SLEEVE 28

38

26

SKIRT

BODICE 12

BODICE 12

65

17

82

⑦ SKIRT

HAND-STITCH, DRAW THE THREAD

1cm

FASTEN TO THE BODY SLIGHTLY ABOVE THE PETTICOAT WAIST LINE

FOLD 0.5 cm TWICE, FINISH WITH SLIP-STITCH

⑧ SLEEVE

2cm

HAND-STITCH

1cm

1cm

2cm

PUT ON ARM, DRAW UP THE STITCHED THREAD

GATHER AND SEW ON BODY

⑨ BODICE

HAND-STITCH

4 cm

1cm

(WRONG SIDE)

FRONT

DRAW UP THE THREAD, FITTING TO THE NECK

⑩ VEST

BACK

TURN IN FRONT BODICE, STEADY WITH SLIP-STITCH

SECURE WITH GLUE

HOOD

⑪ CUTTING GUIDE (VERMILION FELT)

16

FOLD

CROWN FRONT EDGE

15

NECK SIDE

5

11

1 FRILL

OUT-EDGE

4

3

39

3

2 STRINGS

1

25

⑫ SEWING

3cm 1cm

FOLD

(WRONG SIDE)

0.6cm

PUT GATHERINGS, SECURE WITH STEADY-MACHINE

MACHINE

0.3cm

(RIGHT SIDE)

SEW ON

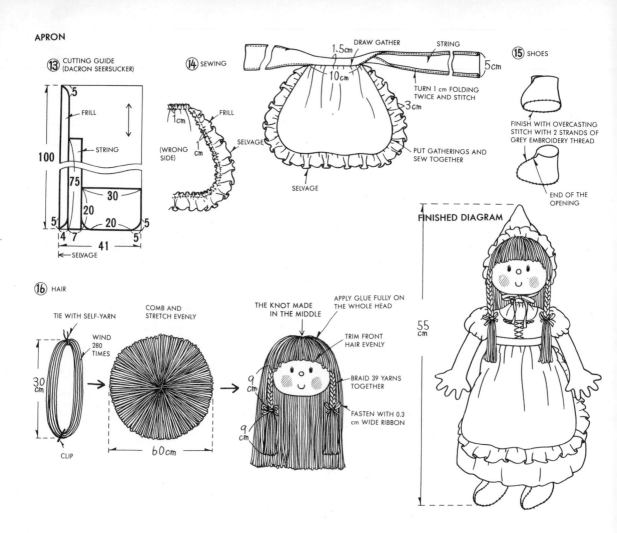

APRON

⑬ CUTTING GUIDE (DACRON SEERSUCKER)

FRILL
STRING
100
75
30
20
20
5
5
4 7
41
SELVAGE
5

⑭ SEWING

DRAW GATHER
STRING
1.5cm
10cm
3cm
TURN 1 cm FOLDING TWICE AND STITCH
5cm

FRILL
1cm
(WRONG SIDE)
1cm
SELVAGE
SELVAGE
PUT GATHERINGS AND SEW TOGETHER

⑮ SHOES

FINISH WITH OVERCASTING STITCH WITH 2 STRANDS OF GREY EMBROIDERY THREAD

END OF THE OPENING

⑯ HAIR

TIE WITH SELF-YARN
COMB AND STRETCH EVENLY
WIND 280 TIMES
30 cm
CLIP
60cm

THE KNOT MADE IN THE MIDDLE
APPLY GLUE FULLY ON THE WHOLE HEAD
TRIM FRONT HAIR EVENLY
9 cm
9 cm
BRAID 39 YARNS TOGETHER
FASTEN WITH 0.3 cm WIDE RIBBON

FINISHED DIAGRAM
55 cm

CARLEN

Shown on page 2.

The hat on her head is a ready-made one. You may knit with raffia yarn, adjusting to her head shape (refer to page 155). Felt fabric is also available as a shoes material.

YOU'LL NEED:
Head-Foundation, Body, Hands, Legs—90 cm by 60 cm White rayon. Face, Nose, Hands, Breastplate—65 cm by 30 cm cotton jersey. Legs—22 cm by 37 cm bleached cotton. Eyes—Dacron georgette. Mouth—Stranded embroidery thread. Hair—Mohair yarn. Bloomer, Petticoat—80 cm by 51 cm White dacron georgette. 145 cm of 5.5 cm lace. Dress—90 cm by 240 cm nylon lace fabric. 26 cm by 20 cm bleached cotton. 100 cm of 0.7 cm satin ribbon. Shoes—21 cm by 10 cm Red suede. And Others—Packing. Cotton wadding. Polyester batting. Hat for interior.

FINISHED SIZE: Refer to diagram.
MAKING INSTRUCTIONS:
The basic manner is same as for Hiji, so make referring to page 50–64.
Finish the openings of legs in same manner as hand.
Put bodice on the body, laying bleached cotton underneath. Sew on sleeves and skirt with the fabric folded in half.
Put skirt with its seam lines laied on center in back, sides in front.
Attach hair in same manner as the hair shown on page 72, trim front hair evenly.

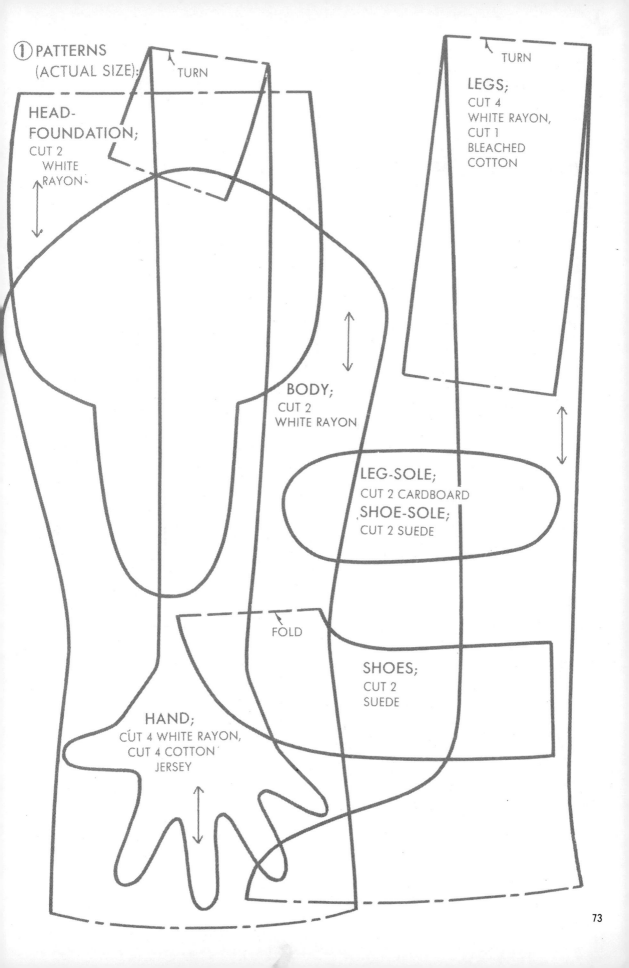

① PATTERNS
(ACTUAL SIZE):

TURN

HEAD-
FOUNDATION;
CUT 2
WHITE
RAYON

LEGS;
CUT 4
WHITE RAYON,
CUT 1
BLEACHED
COTTON

TURN

BODY;
CUT 2
WHITE RAYON

LEG-SOLE;
CUT 2 CARDBOARD

SHOE-SOLE;
CUT 2 SUEDE

FOLD

SHOES;
CUT 2
SUEDE

HAND;
CUT 4 WHITE RAYON,
CUT 4 COTTON
JERSEY

BODY

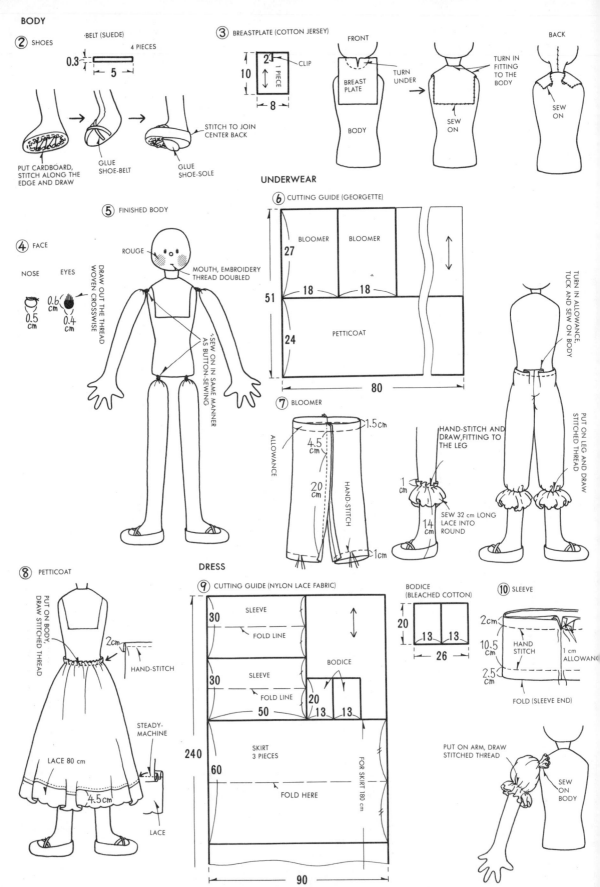

② SHOES · BELT (SUEDE)   4 PIECES
0.3
5

PUT CARDBOARD, STITCH ALONG THE EDGE AND DRAW
GLUE SHOE-BELT
GLUE SHOE-SOLE
STITCH TO JOIN CENTER BACK

③ BREASTPLATE (COTTON JERSEY)
21
10
1 PIECE
CLIP
8

FRONT   BACK
BREAST PLATE
BODY
TURN UNDER
TURN IN FITTING TO THE BODY
SEW ON
SEW ON

④ FACE
NOSE   EYES
0.6 cm
0.5 cm   0.4 cm
DRAW OUT THE THREAD WOVEN CROSSWISE

⑤ FINISHED BODY
ROUGE
MOUTH, EMBROIDERY THREAD DOUBLED
SEW ON IN SAME MANNER AS BUTTON-SEWING

UNDERWEAR

⑥ CUTTING GUIDE (GEORGETTE)
27   BLOOMER   BLOOMER
51   18   18
24   PETTICOAT
80

TURN IN ALLOWANCE, TUCK AND SEW ON BODY
PUT ON LEG AND DRAW STITCHED THREAD

⑦ BLOOMER
1.5 cm
4.5 cm
ALLOWANCE
20 cm
HAND-STITCH
1 cm

HAND-STITCH AND DRAW, FITTING TO THE LEG
1 cm
14 cm
SEW 32 cm LONG LACE INTO ROUND

⑧ PETTICOAT
PUT ON BODY, DRAW STITCHED THREAD
2cm
HAND-STITCH
STEADY-MACHINE
LACE 80 cm
4.5cm
LACE

DRESS

⑨ CUTTING GUIDE (NYLON LACE FABRIC)
30   SLEEVE
FOLD LINE
30   SLEEVE
FOLD LINE
50
240
SKIRT 3 PIECES
60
FOLD HERE
BODICE
20   13   13
FOR SKIRT 180 cm
90

BODICE (BLEACHED COTTON)
20   13   13
26

⑩ SLEEVE
2cm
10.5 cm
HAND STITCH
1 cm ALLOWANCE
2.5 cm
FOLD (SLEEVE END)

PUT ON ARM, DRAW STITCHED THREAD
SEW ON BODY

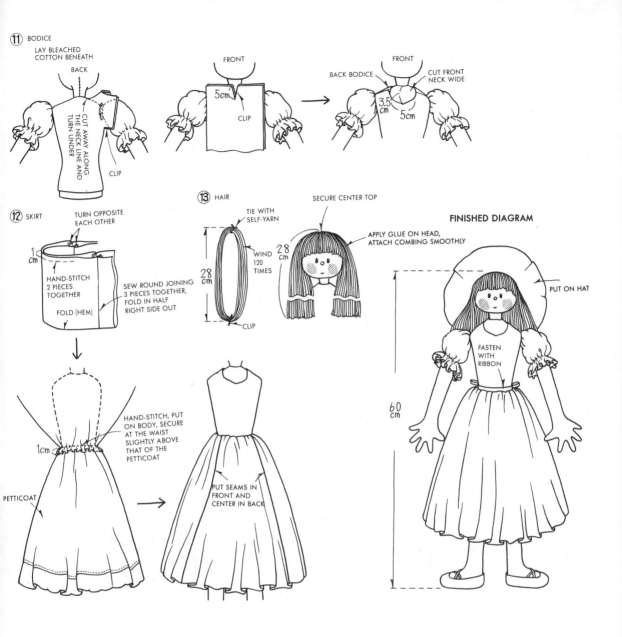

⑪ BODICE

LAY BLEACHED COTTON BENEATH

BACK

CUT AWAY ALONG THE NECK LINE AND TURN UNDER

CLIP

FRONT

5cm

CLIP

FRONT

BACK BODICE

CUT FRONT NECK WIDE

3.5 cm

5cm

⑫ SKIRT

TURN OPPOSITE EACH OTHER

1 cm

HAND-STITCH 2 PIECES TOGETHER

FOLD (HEM)

SEW ROUND JOINING 3 PIECES TOGETHER, FOLD IN HALF RIGHT SIDE OUT

⑬ HAIR

TIE WITH SELF-YARN

WIND 120 TIMES

28 cm

28 cm

CLIP

SECURE CENTER TOP

APPLY GLUE ON HEAD, ATTACH COMBING SMOOTHLY

FINISHED DIAGRAM

HAND-STITCH, PUT ON BODY, SECURE AT THE WAIST SLIGHTLY ABOVE THAT OF THE PETTICOAT

1cm

PETTICOAT

PUT SEAMS IN FRONT AND CENTER IN BACK

PUT ON HAT

FASTEN WITH RIBBON

60 cm

A SMALL HOUSE IN THE FOREST

Shown on page 4–5.

Use fabrics of native cotton to put an atomosphere of the time of American pioneers. Pay attention to the combination of colors on the three girls' wearing apparel.

(MARy)
YOU'LL NEED:
Head-Foundation, Booy, Hands, Legs—90 cm by 18 cm White rayon. Face, Nose, Hands—32 cm by 17 cm Beige cotton jersey. Legs—28 cm Black cotton jersey. Eyes—Dacron georgette. Mouth—Stranded embroidery thread. Hair—Mohair yarn. Bloomer, Petticoat—65 cm by 15 cm White rayon. Skirt, Sleeves, Hood—63 cm by 30 cm denim. Apron-Dress—46 cm by 24 cm cotton print. Shoes—12 cm by 6 cm felt. And Others—Packing. Cotton wadding. Polyester batting.

FINISHED SIZE: Refer to diagram.
MAKING INSTRUCTIONS:
The basic manner is same as for Hiji, so make referring to page 50–64.
Make legs in same manner as hand.
Seam both sides of apron dress, press seams open, finish the hem.
Put hairs on head and secure center on top, glue to steady combing smoothly.
Make shoes following to the size of foot.

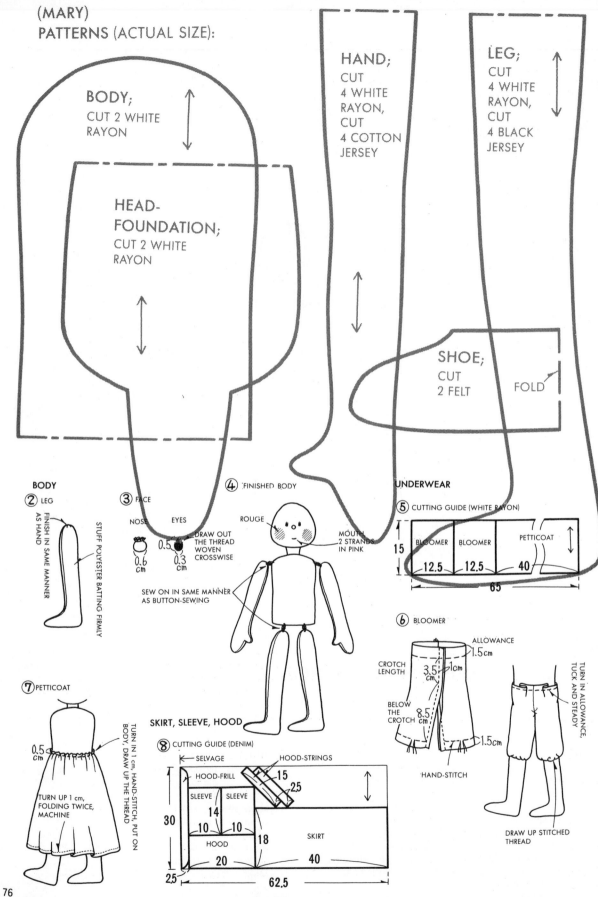

(MARY)
PATTERNS (ACTUAL SIZE):

BODY;
CUT 2 WHITE
RAYON

HEAD-
FOUNDATION;
CUT 2 WHITE
RAYON

HAND;
CUT
4 WHITE
RAYON,
CUT
4 COTTON
JERSEY

LEG;
CUT
4 WHITE
RAYON,
CUT
4 BLACK
JERSEY

SHOE;
CUT
2 FELT

FOLD

BODY

② LEG

FINISH IN SAME MANNER AS HAND

STUFF POLYESTER BATTING FIRMLY

③ FACE

NOSE   EYES

0.6 cm

0.5   0.3 cm

DRAW OUT THE THREAD WOVEN CROSSWISE

SEW ON IN SAME MANNER AS BUTTON-SEWING

④ FINISHED BODY

ROUGE

MOUTH
2 STRANDS
IN PINK

UNDERWEAR

⑤ CUTTING GUIDE (WHITE RAYON)

BLOOMER	BLOOMER	PETTICOAT
12.5	12.5	40

15

65

⑥ BLOOMER

ALLOWANCE
1.5cm

CROTCH
LENGTH   3.5 cm   1cm

BELOW
THE
CROTCH   8.5 cm

1.5cm

HAND-STITCH

TURN IN ALLOWANCE, TUCK AND STEADY

DRAW UP STITCHED THREAD

⑦ PETTICOAT

0.5 cm

TURN IN 1 cm, HAND-STITCH, PUT ON BODY, DRAW UP THE THREAD

TURN UP 1 cm, FOLDING TWICE, MACHINE

SKIRT, SLEEVE, HOOD

⑧ CUTTING GUIDE (DENIM)

SELVAGE

HOOD-FRILL

HOOD-STRINGS

15

2.5

SLEEVE   SLEEVE

14

10   10

HOOD

30

18

SKIRT

20   40

25   62.5

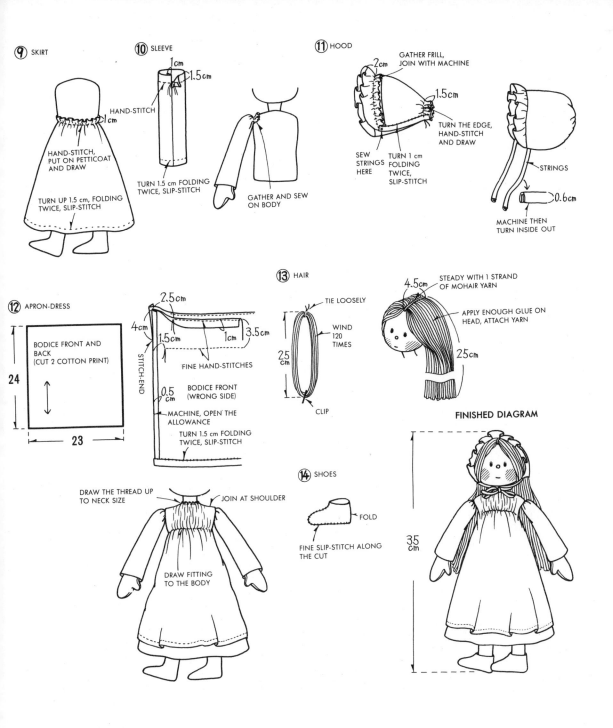

⑨ SKIRT

HAND-STITCH

1 cm

HAND-STITCH, PUT ON PETTICOAT AND DRAW

TURN UP 1.5 cm, FOLDING TWICE, SLIP-STITCH

⑩ SLEEVE

1 cm

1.5 cm

HAND-STITCH

TURN 1.5 cm FOLDING TWICE, SLIP-STITCH

GATHER AND SEW ON BODY

⑪ HOOD

2cm

GATHER FRILL, JOIN WITH MACHINE

1.5 cm

TURN THE EDGE, HAND-STITCH AND DRAW

SEW STRINGS HERE

TURN 1 cm FOLDING TWICE, SLIP-STITCH

STRINGS

0.6cm

MACHINE THEN TURN INSIDE OUT

⑫ APRON-DRESS

BODICE FRONT AND BACK (CUT 2 COTTON PRINT)

24

23

2.5 cm

4 cm

1.5 cm

1 cm

3.5 cm

STITCH-END

FINE HAND-STITCHES

0.5 cm

BODICE FRONT (WRONG SIDE)

MACHINE, OPEN THE ALLOWANCE

TURN 1.5 cm FOLDING TWICE, SLIP-STITCH

⑬ HAIR

TIE LOOSELY

WIND 120 TIMES

25 cm

CLIP

4.5cm

STEADY WITH 1 STRAND OF MOHAIR YARN

APPLY ENOUGH GLUE ON HEAD, ATTACH YARN

25cm

FINISHED DIAGRAM

DRAW THE THREAD UP TO NECK SIZE

JOIN AT SHOULDER

DRAW FITTING TO THE BODY

⑭ SHOES

FOLD

FINE SLIP-STITCH ALONG THE CUT

35 cm

(ROLA)

YOU'LL NEED:
Head-Foundation, Body, Hands, Legs—84 cm by 17 cm White rayon. Face, Nose, Hands—32 cm by 15 cm Beige cotton jersey. Legs—26 cm by 17 cm Black cotton jersey. Eyes—Dacron georgette. Mouth—Stranded embroidery thread. Hair—Mohair yarn. Bloomer, Petticoat—65 cm by 14 cm White rayon. Skirt—50 cm by 16 cm light weight cotton fabric.

Dress, Hood—67 cm by 30 cm cotton print. Shoes—11 cm by 5.5 cm felt. And Others—Packing. Cotton wadding. Polyester batting.

FINISHED SIZE: Refer to diagram.

MAKING INSTRUCTIONS:
The basic manner is same as for Hiji, so make referring to page 50–64.
Make in same manner as for Mary.
Secure hair on top left side, cut the end evenly.

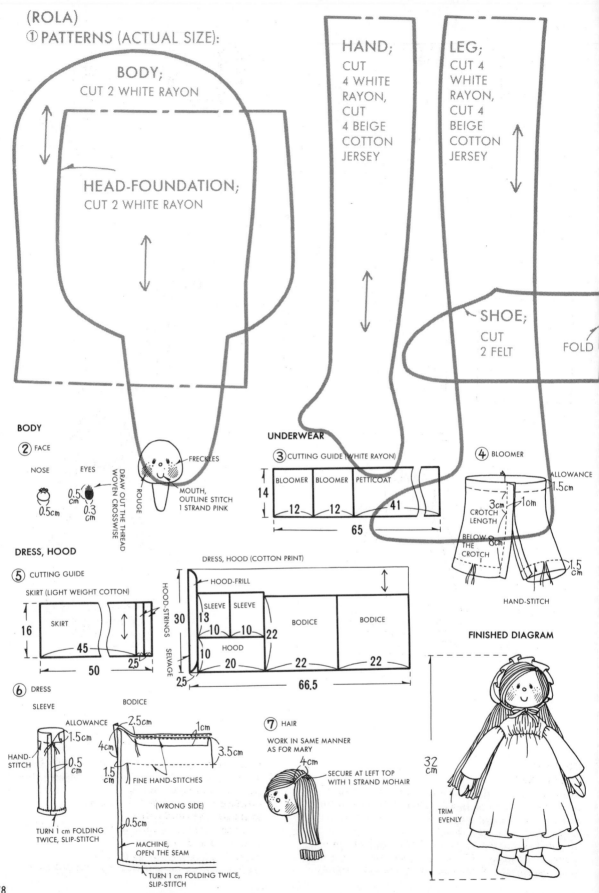

(ROLA)
① PATTERNS (ACTUAL SIZE):

BODY;
CUT 2 WHITE RAYON

HEAD-FOUNDATION;
CUT 2 WHITE RAYON

HAND;
CUT
4 WHITE
RAYON,
CUT
4 BEIGE
COTTON
JERSEY

LEG;
CUT 4
WHITE
RAYON,
CUT 4
BEIGE
COTTON
JERSEY

SHOE;
CUT
2 FELT

FOLD

BODY

② FACE

NOSE

EYES

0.5
cm

0.5cm 0.3cm

DRAW OUT THE THREAD
WOVEN CROSSWISE

ROUGE

FRECKLES

MOUTH,
OUTLINE STITCH
1 STRAND PINK

UNDERWEAR

③ Cutting guide (WHITE RAYON)

14

BLOOMER BLOOMER PETTICOAT

12   12   41

65

④ BLOOMER

ALLOWANCE
1.5cm

3cm   10m
CROTCH
LENGTH

BELOW 8cm
THE
CROTCH

1.5
cm

HAND-STITCH

DRESS, HOOD

⑤ CUTTING GUIDE

SKIRT (LIGHT WEIGHT COTTON)

16

SKIRT

45

50   2.5

DRESS, HOOD (COTTON PRINT)

HOOD-FRILL

SELVAGE   HOOD-STRINGS

30   13 SLEEVE SLEEVE

10   10   22

10   HOOD

25   20   22   22

66.5

FINISHED DIAGRAM

⑥ DRESS

SLEEVE

ALLOWANCE
1.5cm

HAND-
STITCH

0.5
cm

TURN 1 cm FOLDING
TWICE, SLIP-STITCH

BODICE

2.5cm   1cm

4cm

3.5cm

1.5
cm

FINE HAND-STITCHES

(WRONG SIDE)

0.5cm

MACHINE,
OPEN THE SEAM

TURN 1 cm FOLDING TWICE,
SLIP-STITCH

⑦ HAIR

WORK IN SAME MANNER
AS FOR MARY

4cm

SECURE AT LEFT TOP
WITH 1 STRAND MOHAIR

32
cm

TRIM
EVENLY

(CARRY)

YOU'LL NEED:

Head-Foundation, Body, Hands, Legs—60 cm by 12 cm White rayon. Face, Nose, Hands, Legs—30 cm by 20 cm cotton jersey. Eyes—Dacron georgette. Mouth—Stranded embroidery thread. Hair—Mohair yarn. Shoes—6.5 cm by 4.5 cm felt. Bloomer, Petticoat—40 cm by 9 cm White rayon. Skirt—25 cm by 10 cm light weight cotton fabric. Dress, Hood—35 cm by 30 cm cotton print. And Others—Packing. Cotton wadding. Polyester batting.

FINISHED SIZE: Refer to diagram.

MAKING INSTRUCTIONS:

The basic manner is same as for Hiji, so make referring to page 50–64.

Put on shoes and stitch, fitting to each foot.

Make underwear, dress, and hood in same manner as for Mary, put them on.

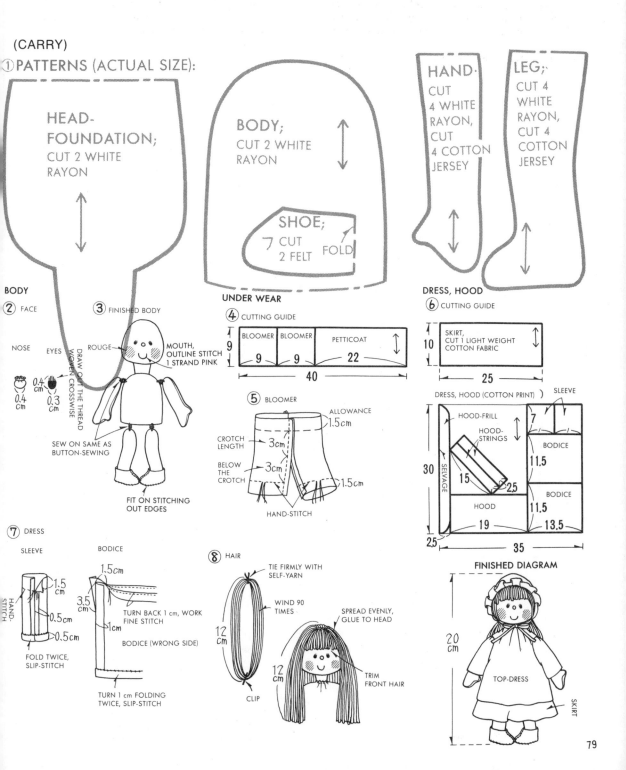

(CARRY)

① PATTERNS (ACTUAL SIZE):

HEAD-FOUNDATION; CUT 2 WHITE RAYON

BODY; CUT 2 WHITE RAYON

SHOE; CUT 2 FELT — FOLD

HAND; CUT 4 WHITE RAYON, CUT 4 COTTON JERSEY

LEG; CUT 4 WHITE RAYON, CUT 4 COTTON JERSEY

BODY

② FACE

NOSE   EYES   ROUGE

MOUTH, OUTLINE STITCH 1 STRAND PINK

0.4 cm   0.4 cm   0.3 cm

DRAW OUT THE THREAD WOVEN CROSSWISE

SEW ON SAME AS BUTTON-SEWING

③ FINISHED BODY

FIT ON STITCHING OUT EDGES

UNDER WEAR

④ CUTTING GUIDE

BLOOMER	BLOOMER	PETTICOAT
9	9	22

9 · 40

⑤ BLOOMER

ALLOWANCE 1.5 cm

CROTCH LENGTH — 3cm

BELOW THE CROTCH — 3cm

1.5 cm

HAND-STITCH

DRESS, HOOD

⑥ CUTTING GUIDE

SKIRT, CUT 1 LIGHT WEIGHT COTTON FABRIC

10 · 25

DRESS, HOOD (COTTON PRINT)

HOOD-FRILL

HOOD-STRINGS

SLEEVE   7

BODICE   11.5

SELVAGE   15   2.5

HOOD   19   13.5

BODICE   11.5

30   2.5   35

⑦ DRESS

SLEEVE

1.5 cm   HAND-STITCH   0.5 cm   0.5 cm

FOLD TWICE, SLIP-STITCH

BODICE

1.5cm   3.5cm   1cm

TURN BACK 1 cm, WORK FINE STITCH

BODICE (WRONG SIDE)

TURN 1 cm FOLDING TWICE, SLIP-STITCH

⑧ HAIR

TIE FIRMLY WITH SELF-YARN

WIND 90 TIMES

12 cm   12 cm

CLIP

SPREAD EVENLY, GLUE TO HEAD

TRIM FRONT HAIR

FINISHED DIAGRAM

20 cm

TOP-DRESS

SKIRT

79

LITTLE WOMEN

Shown on page 6–7.

Very pretty hug-dolls. Four Girls are made in the same way. Feature them using various print fabrics. The hair requires longer length, so use wool yarn if available.

YOU'LL NEED:
Head-Foundation, Body, Hands, Legs—55 cm by 45 cm White rayon. Face, Nose, Hands, Legs—70 cm by 38 cm cotton jersey. Eyes—Dacron georgette. Mouth—Stranded embroidery thread. Hair—Frizzy yarn. Dress, Bloomer, Ribbon—67 cm by 44 cm cotton print. And Others—Packing. Cotton wadding. Polyester batting.
FINISHED SIZE: Refer to diagram.

MAKING INSTRUCTIONS:
The basic manner is same as for Hiji, so make referring to page 50–64.
Sew bloomer, sleeves, and bodice on body in turn. Fasten the yarns for hair in the middle, secure to top of head. Apply glue on the head, attach the yarns parted on side, combing smoothly.
Put ribbon on top head.

① PATTERNS (ACTUAL SIZE):

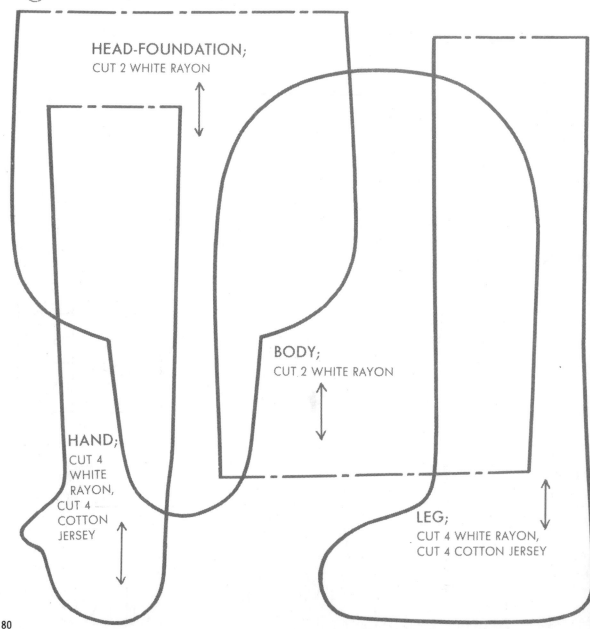

HEAD-FOUNDATION;
CUT 2 WHITE RAYON

BODY;
CUT 2 WHITE RAYON

HAND;
CUT 4 WHITE RAYON, CUT 4 COTTON JERSEY

LEG;
CUT 4 WHITE RAYON, CUT 4 COTTON JERSEY

BODY

② FACE

③ FINISHED BODY

DRESS, BLOOMER, RIBBON

④ CUTTING GUIDE (COTTON PRINT)

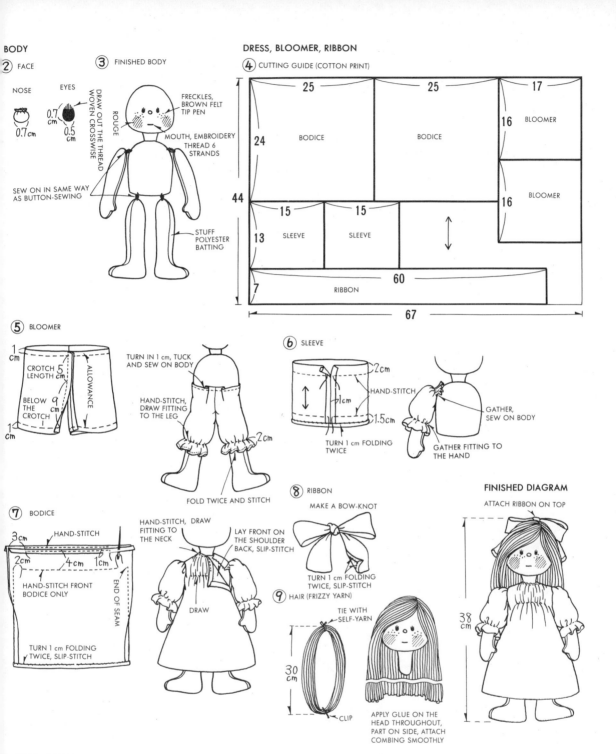

NOSE

0.7cm

EYES

0.7 cm 0.5 cm

DRAW OUT THE THREAD WOVEN CROSSWISE

ROUGE

FRECKLES, BROWN FELT TIP PEN

MOUTH, EMBROIDERY THREAD 6 STRANDS

SEW ON IN SAME WAY AS BUTTON-SEWING

STUFF POLYESTER BATTING

25   25   17

24   BODICE   BODICE   16   BLOOMER

44   16   BLOOMER

15   15

13   SLEEVE   SLEEVE

7   60   RIBBON

67

⑤ BLOOMER

1 cm

CROTCH LENGTH 5 cm   5 cm   ALLOWANCE

BELOW THE CROTCH   9 cm

1 cm

TURN IN 1 cm, TUCK AND SEW ON BODY

HAND-STITCH, DRAW FITTING TO THE LEG

2cm

FOLD TWICE AND STITCH

⑥ SLEEVE

2cm

1cm

HAND-STITCH

1.5cm

TURN 1 cm FOLDING TWICE

GATHER, SEW ON BODY

GATHER FITTING TO THE HAND

⑦ BODICE

3cm   HAND-STITCH

2cm   4cm   1cm

HAND-STITCH FRONT BODICE ONLY

END OF SEAM

TURN 1 cm FOLDING TWICE, SLIP-STITCH

HAND-STITCH, DRAW FITTING TO THE NECK

LAY FRONT ON THE SHOULDER BACK, SLIP-STITCH

DRAW

⑧ RIBBON

MAKE A BOW-KNOT

TURN 1 cm FOLDING TWICE, SLIP-STITCH

⑨ HAIR (FRIZZY YARN)

TIE WITH SELF-YARN

30 cm

CLIP

APPLY GLUE ON THE HEAD THROUGHOUT, PART ON SIDE, ATTACH COMBING SMOOTHLY

FINISHED DIAGRAM

ATTACH RIBBON ON TOP

38 cm

MOTHER GOOSE

Shown on page 8–9.

Bodies are simply set up using scraps of fabric. Make expressive dolls following to the taste of each child.

(MONDAY'S CHILD)

YOU'LL NEED:

Head-Foundation—24 cm by 18 cm White rayon. Face, Nose—24 cm by 22 cm cotton jersey. Body, Hands, Skirt, Collar—21 cm by 75 cm velveteen. 110 cm of 1 cm lace. Eyes—Dacron georgette. Mouth—Stranded embroidery thread. Hair—Mohair yarn. 30 cm of 1 cm ribbon. And Others—Artificial flowers. Packing. Cotton wadding. Polyester batting.

MAKING INSTRUCTIONS:

The basic manner is same as for Hiji, so make referring to page 50–64.

Make head-foundation, face in the same way as for Hiji.

Cut out body, hands, skirt, and collar from veleveteen.

Sew body leaving the opening for stuffing on back, stuff packing into the top where neck to be fixed as firm as possible. Then stuff polyester batting from the toe carefully.

Sew hand, make a slash on the hand inward, turn inside out and stuff polyester batting.

Make a neck-size hole on the top of the body, apply glue, insert neck into steadily.

Attach hair following to the manner shown on page 72.

*Use patterns below for all children here. Make head and body in the same manner.

① PATTERNS (ACTUAL SIZE):

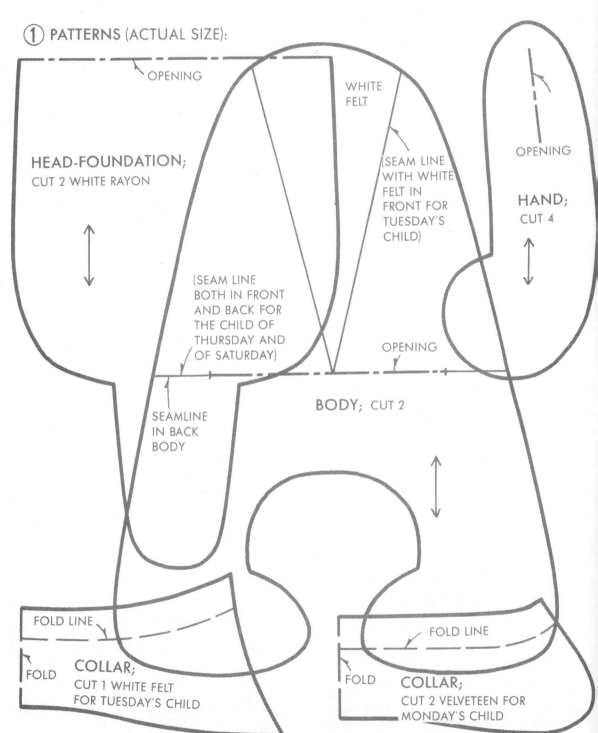

OPENING

WHITE FELT

(SEAM LINE WITH WHITE FELT IN FRONT FOR TUESDAY'S CHILD)

OPENING

HAND; CUT 4

HEAD-FOUNDATION; CUT 2 WHITE RAYON

(SEAM LINE BOTH IN FRONT AND BACK FOR THE CHILD OF THURSDAY AND OF SATURDAY)

OPENING

SEAMLINE IN BACK BODY

BODY; CUT 2

FOLD LINE

FOLD

COLLAR; CUT 1 WHITE FELT FOR TUESDAY'S CHILD

FOLD LINE

FOLD

COLLAR; CUT 2 VELVETEEN FOR MONDAY'S CHILD

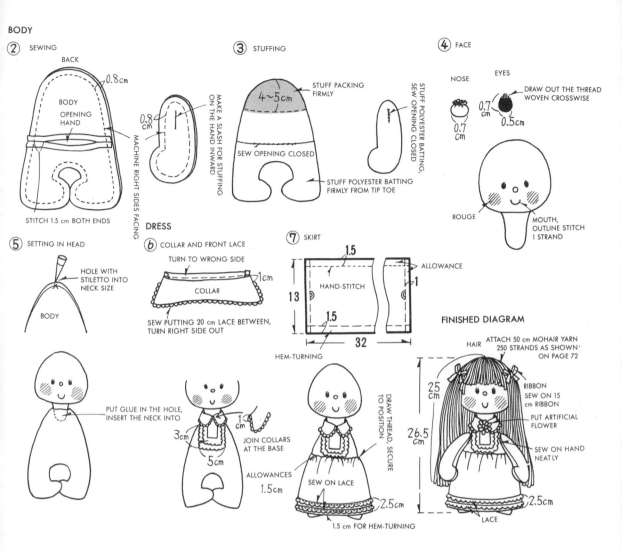

BODY

② SEWING

BACK

0.8 cm

BODY OPENING HAND

MACHINE RIGHT SIDES FACING

STITCH 1.5 cm BOTH ENDS

0.8 cm

MAKE A SLASH FOR STUFFING ON THE HAND INWARD

③ STUFFING

STUFF PACKING FIRMLY

4~5cm

SEW OPENING CLOSED

STUFF POLYESTER BATTING, SEW OPENING CLOSED

STUFF POLYESTER BATTING FIRMLY FROM TIP TOE

④ FACE

NOSE

EYES

DRAW OUT THE THREAD WOVEN CROSSWISE

0.7 cm

0.7 0.5 cm

0.7 cm

ROUGE

MOUTH, OUTLINE STITCH 1 STRAND

⑤ SETTING IN HEAD

HOLE WITH STILETTO INTO NECK SIZE

BODY

DRESS

⑥ COLLAR AND FRONT LACE

TURN TO WRONG SIDE

1cm

COLLAR

SEW PUTTING 20 cm LACE BETWEEN, TURN RIGHT SIDE OUT

⑦ SKIRT

1.5

HAND-STITCH

ALLOWANCE

1

13

1.5

32

HEM-TURNING

PUT GLUE IN THE HOLE, INSERT THE NECK INTO

1 cm

3cm

5cm

JOIN COLLARS AT THE BASE

ALLOWANCES

1.5cm

DRAW THREAD, SECURE TO POSITION

SEW ON LACE

1.5 cm FOR HEM-TURNING

2.5cm

FINISHED DIAGRAM

HAIR

ATTACH 50 cm MOHAIR YARN 250 STRANDS AS SHOWN ON PAGE 72

25 cm

26.5 cm

RIBBON SEW ON 15 cm RIBBON

PUT ARTIFICIAL FLOWER

SEW ON HAND NEATLY

LACE

2.5cm

(TUESDAY'S CHILD)

YOU'LL NEED:

Head-Foundation—24 cm by 18 cm White rayon. Face, Nose—24 cm by 22 cm cotton jersey. Body, Hands—42 cm by 24 cm velveteen. Eyes—Dacron georgette. Mouth—Stranded embroidery thread. Hair—Mohair yarn. Collar, Yoke—20 cm by 10 cm felt. And others —6 cm of 5 cm ribbon. Packing. Cotton wadding.

Polyester batting.

MAKING INSTRUCTIONS:

Make in same manner as for Monday's child. Make hairs winding 2 strands of yarns around 2 fingers ten times, tie with White machine thread, secure to head as shown on page 67.

FINISHED DIAGRAM

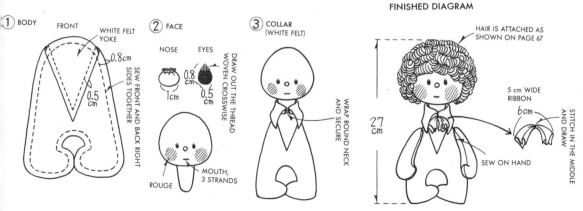

① BODY

FRONT

WHITE FELT YOKE

0.8 cm

0.5 cm

SEW FRONT AND BACK RIGHT SIDES TOGETHER

② FACE

NOSE

EYES

DRAW OUT THE THREAD WOVEN CROSSWISE

1cm

0.8 cm

0.5 cm

MOUTH, 3 STRANDS

ROUGE

③ COLLAR (WHITE FELT)

WRAP ROUND NECK AND SECURE

HAIR IS ATTACHED AS SHOWN ON PAGE 67

27 cm

5 cm WIDE RIBBON

6cm

STITCH IN THE MIDDLE AND DRAW

SEW ON HAND

83

(WEDENSDAY'S CHILD)

YOU'LL NEED:

Head-Foundation—24 cm by 18 cm White rayon. Face, Nose—24 cm by 22 cm cotton jersey. Body, Hands, Skirt—72 cm by 24 cm velveteen. Eyes—Dacron georgette. Mouth—Stranded embroidery thread. Hair—Mohair yarn. Apron, Hood—65 cm by 26 cm light weight cotton fabric. 66 cm of 1.5 cm lace.

And Others—1.3 cm diameter button. 15 cm of 1.5 cm lace. Packing. Cotton wadding. Polyester batting.

MAKING INSTRUCTIONS:

Make in same manner as for Monday's child.
Make hood and apron.
Wrap lace round the neck, secure with button.

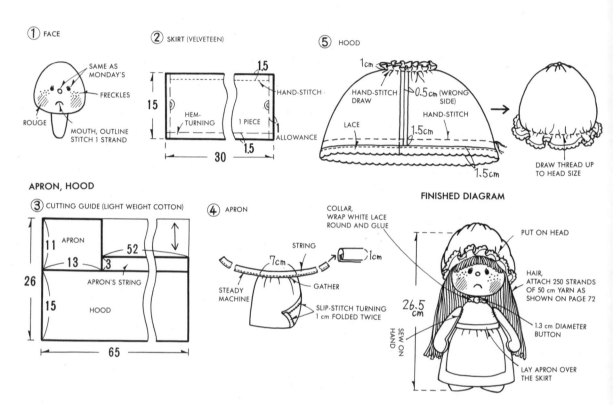

APRON, HOOD

FINISHED DIAGRAM

(THURSDAY'S CHILD)

YOU'LL NEED:

Head-Foundation—24 cm by 18 cm White rayon. Face, Nose—24 cm by 22 cm cotton jersey. Body, Hands—52 cm by 12 cm velveteen. Legs—30 cm by 11 cm corduroy. Eyes—Dacron georgette. Mouth—Stranded embroidery thread. Hair—Mohair yarn. Scarf—15 cm by 15 cm wool. Hood, Suitcase—Heavy weight

yarn. And Others—3 of 0.8 cm diameter button. Packing. Cotton wadding. Polyester batting.

MAKING INSTRUCTIONS:

Make in same manner as for Monday's child.
Crochet hood with No. 5/0 crochet hook, and put on head. Crochet suitcase with the yarn same as hood.

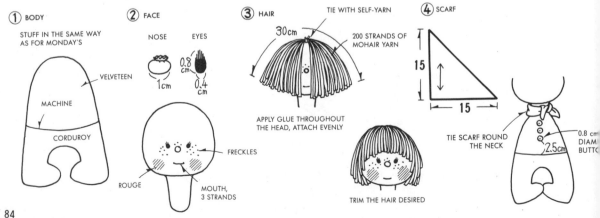

84

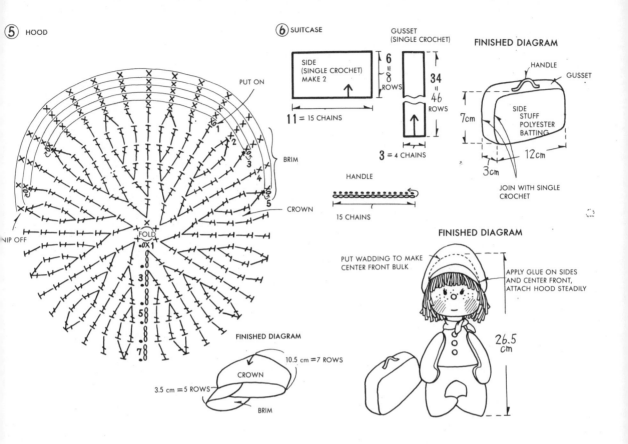

⑤ HOOD

PUT ON

BRIM

CROWN

NIP OFF

FOLD
0 X 1

⑥ SUITCASE

GUSSET
(SINGLE CROCHET)

SIDE
(SINGLE CROCHET)
MAKE 2

6
"
8
ROWS

11 = 15 CHAINS

34
"
46
ROWS

3 = 4 CHAINS

HANDLE

15 CHAINS

FINISHED DIAGRAM

HANDLE

GUSSET

SIDE
STUFF
POLYESTER
BATTING

7cm

12cm

3cm

JOIN WITH SINGLE
CROCHET

FINISHED DIAGRAM

PUT WADDING TO MAKE
CENTER FRONT BULK

APPLY GLUE ON SIDES
AND CENTER FRONT,
ATTACH HOOD STEADILY

26.5
cm

FINISHED DIAGRAM

10.5 cm = 7 ROWS

CROWN

3.5 cm = 5 ROWS

BRIM

(FRIDAY'S CHILD)

YOU'LL NEED:
Head-Foundation—24 cm by 18 cm White rayon.
Face, Nose—24 cm by 22 cm cotton jersey. Body,
Skirt, Hands, Ribbon—80 cm by 19 cm velvetten. Eyes
—Dacron georgette. Mouth—Stranded embroidery
thread. Hair—Mohair yarn. Stole, Hair-Band—Light
weight yarn. And Others—Packing. Cotton wadding.
Polyester batting.

MAKING INSTRUCTIONS:
Make in same manner as for Monday's child.
Crochet hair-band and stole with No. 0 lace hook, put
them on the doll.

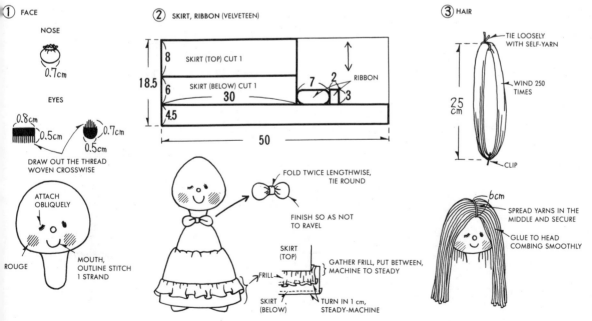

① FACE

NOSE

0.7cm

EYES

0.8cm
0.5cm
0.7cm
0.5cm

DRAW OUT THE THREAD
WOVEN CROSSWISE

ATTACH
OBLIQUELY

ROUGE

MOUTH,
OUTLINE STITCH
1 STRAND

② SKIRT, RIBBON (VELVETEEN)

8   SKIRT (TOP) CUT 1

18.5   6   SKIRT (BELOW) CUT 1
30

7   2   3   RIBBON

4.5

50

FOLD TWICE LENGTHWISE,
TIE ROUND

FINISH SO AS NOT
TO RAVEL

SKIRT
(TOP)

FRILL

SKIRT
(BELOW)

GATHER FRILL, PUT BETWEEN,
MACHINE TO STEADY

TURN IN 1 cm,
STEADY-MACHINE

③ HAIR

TIE LOOSELY
WITH SELF-YARN

WIND 250
TIMES

25
cm

CLIP

6cm

SPREAD YARNS IN THE
MIDDLE AND SECURE

GLUE TO HEAD
COMBING SMOOTHLY

85

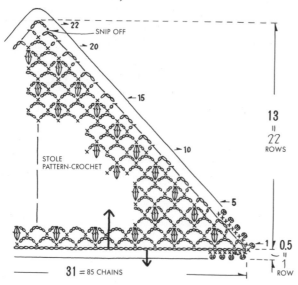

22
SNIP OFF
20
15
STOLE PATTERN-CROCHET
10
5
13 = 22 ROWS
1 0.5
1 ROW
31 = 85 CHAINS

⑤ HAIR-BAND (LIGHT WEIGHT YARN 1 STRAND)

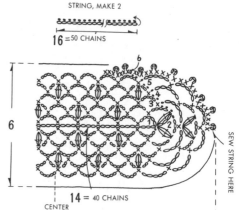

STRING, MAKE 2
16 = 50 CHAINS

6
5
3 4
1 2 8
SEW STRING HERE

14 = 40 CHAINS
CENTER
22

FINISHED DIAGRAM

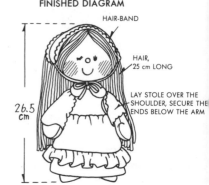

HAIR-BAND
HAIR, 25 cm LONG
26.5 cm
LAY STOLE OVER THE SHOULDER, SECURE THE ENDS BELOW THE ARM

(SATURDAY'S CHILD)

YOU'LL NEED:

Head-Foundation—24 cm by 18 cm White rayon. Face, Nose—24 cm by 22 cm cotton jersey. Body, Hands, Collar—52 cm by 20 cm velveteen. Legs—30 cm by 11 cm striped velveteen. Eyes—Dacron georgette. Mouth—Stranded embroidery thread. Hair—Mohair yarn. And Others—30 cm of 1 cm braid. 30 cm square guaze. Packing. Cotton wadding. Polyester batting.

MAKING INSTRUCTIONS:

Cut out top and pants of the body from different fabric.
Make in same manner as for Monday's child.
Sew hairs of yarn on the head all over, without clipping.

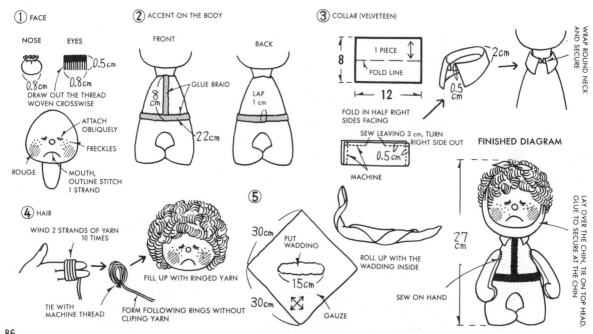

① FACE

NOSE   EYES
0.5 cm
0.8 cm   0.8 cm
DRAW OUT THE THREAD WOVEN CROSSWISE
ATTACH OBLIQUELY
FRECKLES
ROUGE
MOUTH, OUTLINE STITCH 1 STRAND

② ACCENT ON THE BODY
FRONT   BACK
GLUE BRAID
8 cm
LAP 1 cm
22 cm

③ COLLAR (VELVETEEN)
1 PIECE
FOLD LINE
8
12
FOLD IN HALF RIGHT SIDES FACING
SEW LEAVING 3 cm, TURN RIGHT SIDE OUT
0.5 cm
MACHINE
2 cm
0.5 cm
WRAP ROUND NECK AND SECURE

④ HAIR
WIND 2 STRANDS OF YARN 10 TIMES
TIE WITH MACHINE THREAD
FILL UP WITH RINGED YARN
FORM FOLLOWING RINGS WITHOUT CLIPING YARN

⑤
30 cm
PUT WADDING
15 cm
30 cm
GAUZE
ROLL UP WITH THE WADDING INSIDE
SEW ON HAND

FINISHED DIAGRAM
27 cm
LAY OVER THE CHIN, TIE ON TOP HEAD. GLUE TO SECURE AT THE CHIN

(SABBATH DAY'S CHILD)

YOU'LL NEED:

Head-Foundation—24 cm by 18 cm White rayon. Face, Nose—24 cm by 22 cm cotton jersey. Body, Hands, Skirt, Hood—75 cm by 26 cm velveteen. Eyes—Dacron georgette. Mouth—Stranded embroidery thread. Hair—Mohair yarn. Apron—35 cm by 11 cm light weight cotton fabric. And Others—100 cm of 1.5 cm lace. 10 cm of 0.5 cm ribbon. Packing. Cotton wadding. Polyester batting.

MAKING INSTRUCTIONS:

Make in same manner as for Monday's child.
Sew on apron and attach hood.

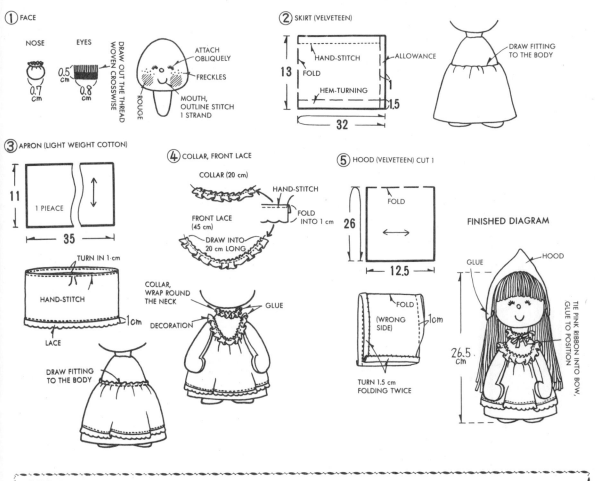

① FACE

NOSE EYES

0.7 cm 0.5 cm 0.8 cm

DRAW OUT THE THREAD WOVEN CROSSWISE

ATTACH OBLIQUELY
FRECKLES
ROUGE
MOUTH, OUTLINE STITCH 1 STRAND

② SKIRT (VELVETEEN)

HAND-STITCH ALLOWANCE
13 FOLD
HEM-TURNING 1.5
32
DRAW FITTING TO THE BODY

③ APRON (LIGHT WEIGHT COTTON)

11 1 PIEACE
35

TURN IN 1 cm
HAND-STITCH
LACE
DRAW FITTING TO THE BODY
1 cm

④ COLLAR, FRONT LACE

COLLAR (20 cm)
HAND-STITCH
FRONT LACE (45 cm)
FOLD INTO 1 cm
DRAW INTO 20 cm LONG
COLLAR, WRAP ROUND THE NECK
DECORATION
GLUE

⑤ HOOD (VELVETEEN) CUT 1

FOLD
26
12.5
FOLD (WRONG SIDE) 1 cm
TURN 1.5 cm FOLDING TWICE

FINISHED DIAGRAM

GLUE HOOD
26.5 cm

TIE THE PINK RIBBON INTO BOW, GLUE TO POSITION

MARIA

Shown on page 10.

Joins are free to move, you may make her pose as you like. The body of such a tall and skinny doll should be finished firmly with packing.

YOU'LL NEED:

Head-Foundation, Body, Hands, Legs—90 cm by 55 cm White rayon. Face, Nose, Hands—90 cm by 30 cm Beige georgette. Legs—70 cm by 27 cm White georgette. Eyes—Dacron georgette. Mouth—Stranded embroidery thread. Hair—Sport weight yarn. Bloomer, Petticoat—85 cm by 34 cm broad cloth. 130 cm of 5 cm lace. Skirt—80 cm by 40 cm cotton print. Apron—28 cm by 35 cm crepe. Sleeves, Bodice—62 cm by 30 cm lace fabric. 80 cm of 3.5 cm lace. Vest—30 cm by 17 cm Black felt. 40 cm of 1 cm Tyrolean braid. Shoes—22 cm by 16 cm light weight cotton fabric 8 cm by 6 cm Brown felt. And Others—Packing. Cotton wadding. Polyester batting.

FINISHED SIZE: 74 cm tall.

MAKING INSTRUCTIONS

The basic manner is same as for Hiji, so make referring to page 50–64.

Make hands and legs to be bent freely.

Cut shoe pieces on bias fabric and sew on.

Sew on bodice front and back neatly. Put on vest in same manner as bodice.

Make hair with yarn, put on head and trim.

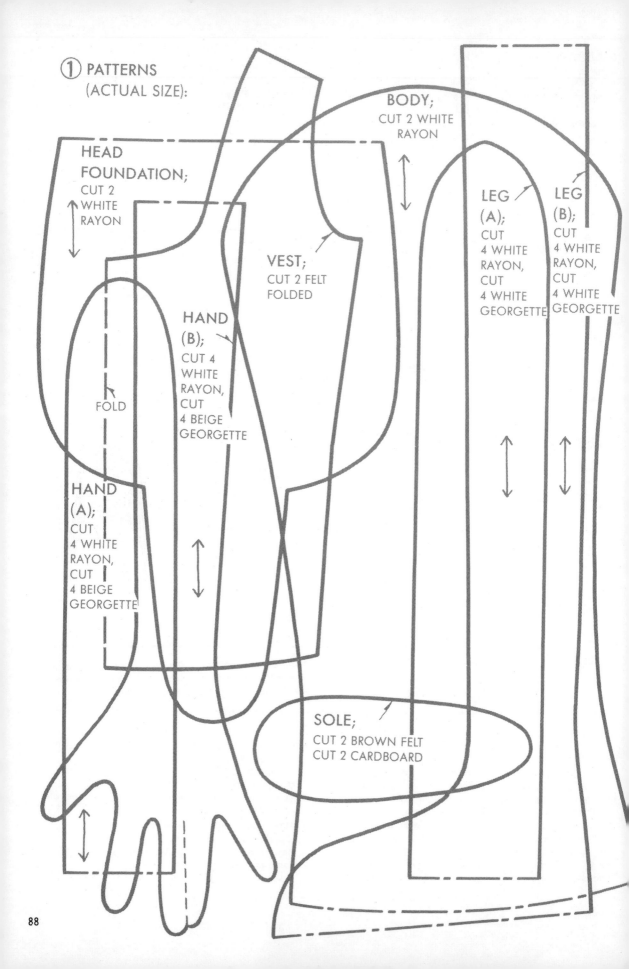

① PATTERNS
(ACTUAL SIZE):

HEAD
FOUNDATION;
CUT 2
WHITE
RAYON

BODY;
CUT 2 WHITE
RAYON

LEG
(A);
CUT
4 WHITE
RAYON,
CUT
4 WHITE
GEORGETTE

LEG
(B);
CUT
4 WHITE
RAYON,
CUT
4 WHITE
GEORGETTE

VEST;
CUT 2 FELT
FOLDED

HAND
(B);
CUT 4
WHITE
RAYON,
CUT
4 BEIGE
GEORGETTE

FOLD

HAND
(A);
CUT
4 WHITE
RAYON,
CUT
4 BEIGE
GEORGETTE

SOLE;
CUT 2 BROWN FELT
CUT 2 CARDBOARD

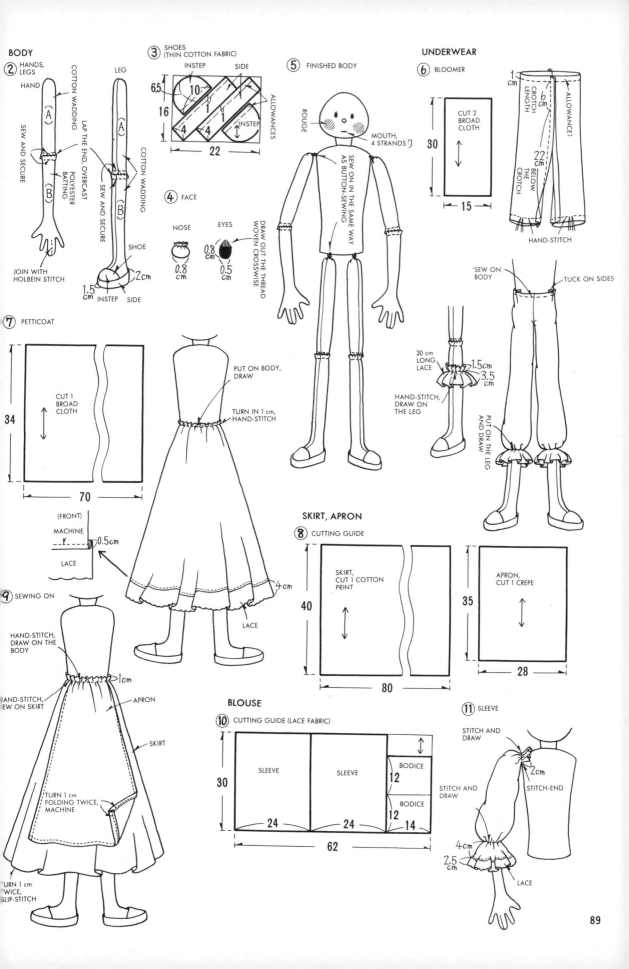

BODY

② HANDS, LEGS

HAND

LEG

COTTON WADDING

A

COTTON WADDING

A

SEW AND SECURE

LAP THE END, OVERCAST

POLYESTER BATTING

B

SEW AND SECURE

B

COTTON WADDING

SHOE

JOIN WITH HOLBEIN STITCH

2cm

1.5 cm

INSTEP SIDE

③ SHOES
(THIN COTTON FABRIC)

INSTEP

SIDE

6.5

10

16

1

1

INSTEP

4   4

ALLOWANCES

22

④ FACE

NOSE

0.8 cm

EYES

0.8 cm

0.5 cm

DRAW OUT THE THREAD WOVEN CROSSWISE

⑤ FINISHED BODY

ROUGE

MOUTH, 4 STRANDS

SEW ON IN THE SAME WAY AS BUTTON-SEWING

⑦ PETTICOAT

CUT 1 BROAD CLOTH

34

70

(FRONT)

MACHINE

0.5cm

LACE

⑨ SEWING ON

HAND-STITCH, DRAW ON THE BODY

1cm

HAND-STITCH, SEW ON SKIRT

APRON

SKIRT

TURN 1 cm FOLDING TWICE, MACHINE

TURN 1 cm TWICE, SLIP-STITCH

PUT ON BODY, DRAW

TURN IN 1 cm, HAND-STITCH

4cm

LACE

UNDERWEAR

⑥ BLOOMER

CUT 2 BROAD CLOTH

30

15

1 cm

CROTCH LENGTH

ALLOWANCE

6 cm

22 cm

BELOW THE CROTCH

HAND-STITCH

SEW ON BODY

TUCK ON SIDES

30 cm LONG LACE

1.5cm

3.5 cm

HAND-STITCH, DRAW ON THE LEG

PUT ON THE LEG AND DRAW

SKIRT, APRON

⑧ CUTTING GUIDE

SKIRT, CUT 1 COTTON PRINT

40

80

APRON, CUT 1 CREPE

35

28

BLOUSE

⑩ CUTTING GUIDE (LACE FABRIC)

SLEEVE

SLEEVE

BODICE

12

BODICE

12

14

30

24   24

62

⑪ SLEEVE

STITCH AND DRAW

2cm

STITCH AND DRAW

STITCH-END

4cm

2.5 cm

LACE

89

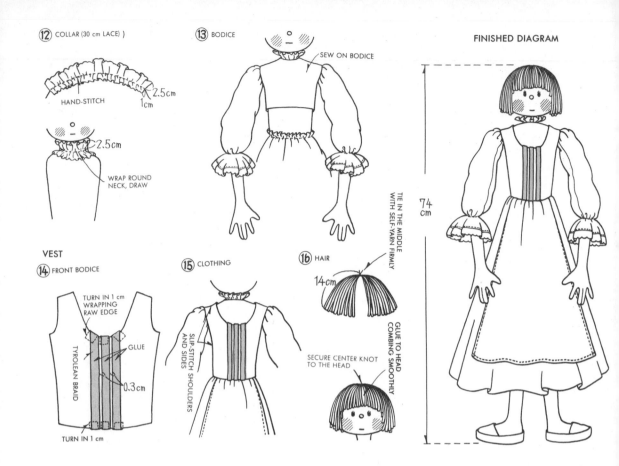

⑫ COLLAR (30 cm LACE))

HAND-STITCH
2.5cm
1cm

2.5cm

WRAP ROUND NECK, DRAW

⑬ BODICE

SEW ON BODICE

FINISHED DIAGRAM

74 cm

VEST

⑭ FRONT BODICE

TURN IN 1 cm WRAPPING RAW EDGE

TYROLEAN BRAID

GLUE

0.3cm

TURN IN 1 cm

⑮ CLOTHING

SLIP-STITCH SHOULDERS AND SIDES

⑯ HAIR

TIE IN THE MIDDLE WITH SELF-YARN FIRMLY

14cm

GLUE TO HEAD COMBING SMOOTHLY

SECURE CENTER KNOT TO THE HEAD

ELLIZA

Shown on page 11.

Use Maria's patterns. Try to image the town of London in winter. Make a carefree girl selling flowers at the market.

YOU'LL NEED:
Head-Foundation, Body, Hands, Legs—90 cm by 55 cm White rayon. Face, Nose, Hands—90 cm by 30 cm Beige georgette. Legs—70 cm by 27 cm Balck woolly nylon. Eyes—Dacron georgette. Mouth—Stranded embroidery thread. Hair—Mohair yarn. Bloomer, Petticoat—85 cm by 34 cm broad cloth. 130 cm of 5 cm lace. Suit—90 cm by 56 cm velveteen. Blouse—46 cm by 34 cm crepe. Apron—80 cm by 40 cm cotton print. Scarf—23 cm by 23 cm georgette. Hat—Black heavy weight yarn. 30 cm of 0.6 cm grosgrain ribbon. Artificial flowers. Stole, Bag—Frizzy yarn. Artificial flower. Shoes—18 cm by 13 cm corduroy. And Others

—Packing. Cotton wadding. Polyester batting.
FINISHED SIZE: Refer to diagram.
MAKING INSTRUCTIONS:
As for the body, use Maria's patterns on page 88, and make referring to the basic manners on page 50–64.
Use Black woolly nylon as a skin fabric of legs.
As for the hair, make 80 cm long skein of yarn and sew on in same manner as for Hiji, braid the yarn on sides.
Crochet hat, sew on a bunch of flowers.
Crochet stole with 1 strand, bag with 2 strands, and put a bunch of flowers in the bag.

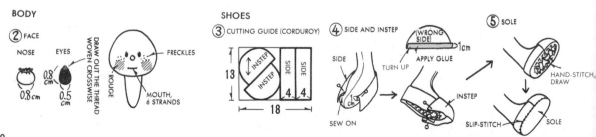

BODY

② FACE

NOSE   EYES
0.8 cm   0.8 cm
0.8cm   0.5 cm

DRAW OUT THE THREAD WOVEN CROSSWISE

FRECKLES

ROUGE

MOUTH, 6 STRANDS

SHOES

③ CUTTING GUIDE (CORDUROY)

INSTEP
INSTEP
SIDE
SIDE
13
4   4
18

④ SIDE AND INSTEP

(WRONG SIDE)
1cm
APPLY GLUE
TURN UP

SIDE

SEW ON
INSTEP

⑤ SOLE

HAND-STITCH DRAW

SLIP-STITCH
SOLE

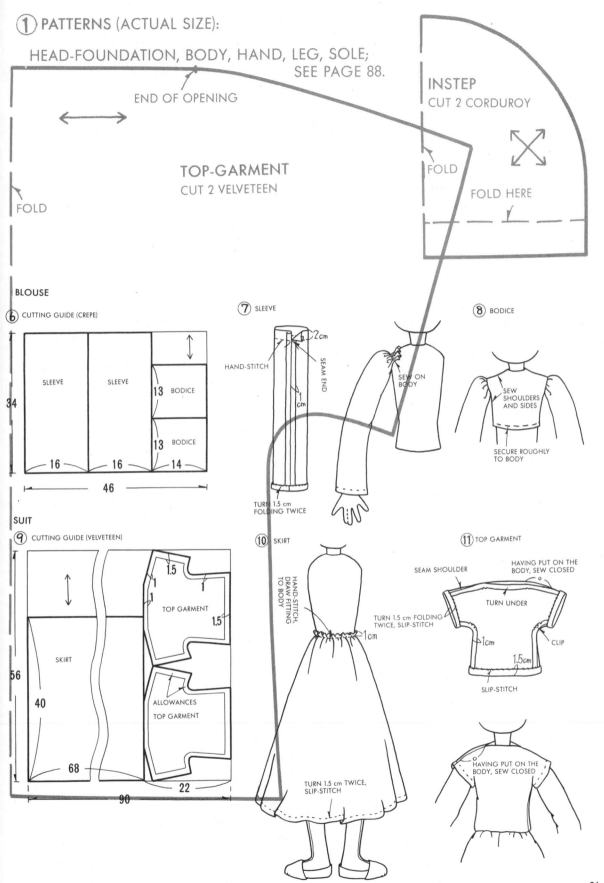

(1) PATTERNS (ACTUAL SIZE):

HEAD-FOUNDATION, BODY, HAND, LEG, SOLE;
SEE PAGE 88.

END OF OPENING

↔

TOP-GARMENT
CUT 2 VELVETEEN

FOLD

INSTEP
CUT 2 CORDUROY

FOLD

FOLD HERE

BLOUSE

(6) CUTTING GUIDE (CREPE)

34

| SLEEVE | SLEEVE | 13 | BODICE |
| | | 13 | BODICE |

16   16   14

46

(7) SLEEVE

2 cm

HAND-STITCH

SEAM END

1 cm

TURN 1.5 cm
FOLDING TWICE

SEW ON
BODY

(8) BODICE

SEW
SHOULDERS
AND SIDES

SECURE ROUGHLY
TO BODY

SUIT

(9) CUTTING GUIDE (VELVETEEN)

1.5
1   1
1   TOP GARMENT
1.5

SKIRT

56

40

ALLOWANCES

TOP GARMENT

68   22

90

(10) SKIRT

HAND-STITCH,
DRAW FITTING
TO BODY

TURN 1.5 cm FOLDING
TWICE, SLIP-STITCH

1 cm

TURN 1.5 cm TWICE,
SLIP-STITCH

(11) TOP GARMENT

SEAM SHOULDER

HAVING PUT ON THE
BODY, SEW CLOSED

TURN UNDER

1 cm

CLIP

1.5 cm

SLIP-STITCH

HAVING PUT ON THE
BODY, SEW CLOSED

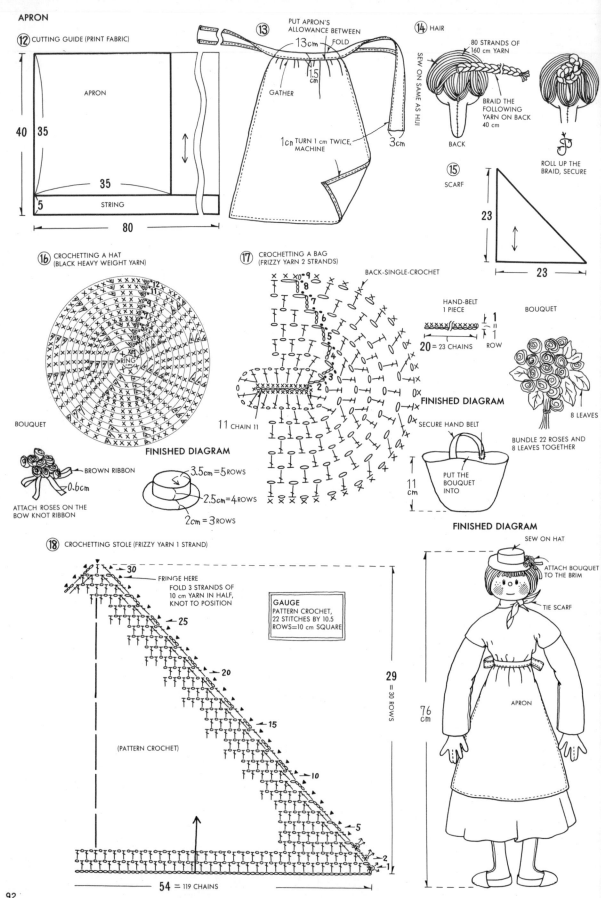

APRON

⑫ CUTTING GUIDE (PRINT FABRIC)

APRON

40
35
35
35
5 STRING
80

⑬ PUT APRON'S ALLOWANCE BETWEEN FOLD
13cm
1.5cm
GATHER
1cm TURN 1 cm TWICE, MACHINE
3cm

SEW ON SAME AS HIJI

⑭ HAIR
80 STRANDS OF 160 cm YARN
BACK
BRAID THE FOLLOWING YARN ON BACK 40 cm
ROLL UP THE BRAID, SECURE

⑮ SCARF
23
23

⑯ CROCHETTING A HAT (BLACK HEAVY WEIGHT YARN)

RING

BOUQUET

BROWN RIBBON
0.6cm

ATTACH ROSES ON THE BOW KNOT RIBBON

FINISHED DIAGRAM
3.5cm = 5 ROWS
2.5cm = 4 ROWS
2cm = 3 ROWS

⑰ CROCHETTING A BAG (FRIZZY YARN 2 STRANDS)

BACK-SINGLE-CROCHET

11 CHAIN 11

HAND-BELT 1 PIECE
1
1
1 ROW
20 = 23 CHAINS

FINISHED DIAGRAM

SECURE HAND BELT

11 cm

PUT THE BOUQUET INTO

FINISHED DIAGRAM

BOUQUET

8 LEAVES

BUNDLE 22 ROSES AND 8 LEAVES TOGETHER

⑱ CROCHETTING STOLE (FRIZZY YARN 1 STRAND)

30
FRINGE HERE
FOLD 3 STRANDS OF 10 cm YARN IN HALF, KNOT TO POSITION

25

20

GAUGE
PATTERN CROCHET,
22 STITCHES BY 10.5
ROWS = 10 cm SQUARE

15

(PATTERN CROCHET)

10

5

2
1

54 = 119 CHAINS

29 = 30 ROWS

76 cm

SEW ON HAT
ATTACH BOUQUET TO THE BRIM
TIE SCARF
APRON

ROZALY

Shown on page 12.

This is a hug-doll easy to be made in the same manner as for Hiji. Use colored tacking thread as hairs, clipping its skein in the middle.

YOU'LL NEED:

Head-Foundation, Body, Hands, Legs—50 cm by 30 cm White rayon. Face, Nose, Hands, Legs—40 cm by 27 cm Beige georgette. Eyes—Dacron georgette. Mouth—Stranded embroidery thread. Hair—3 skeins of Pink tacking thread. 50 cm of 0.5 cm ribbon. Bloomer, Petticoat—65 cm by 13 cm broad cloth. 35 cm of 1.8 cm lace. Skirt, Bodice—45 cm by 60 cm cotton print. Sleeves, Apron—52 cm by 12 cm lawn. 10 cm of 2.5 cm lace. And Others—Packing. Cotton wadding. Polyester batting.

FINISHED SIZE: Refer to diagram.
MAKING INSTRUCTIONS:
The basic manner is same as for Hiji, so make referring to page 50–64.
Make legs stuffing polyester batting, finish in the same way as hand.
Attach hair as shown on page 72.
Use selvage side for the skirt-frill, but if not available, finish cut edges folding twice.

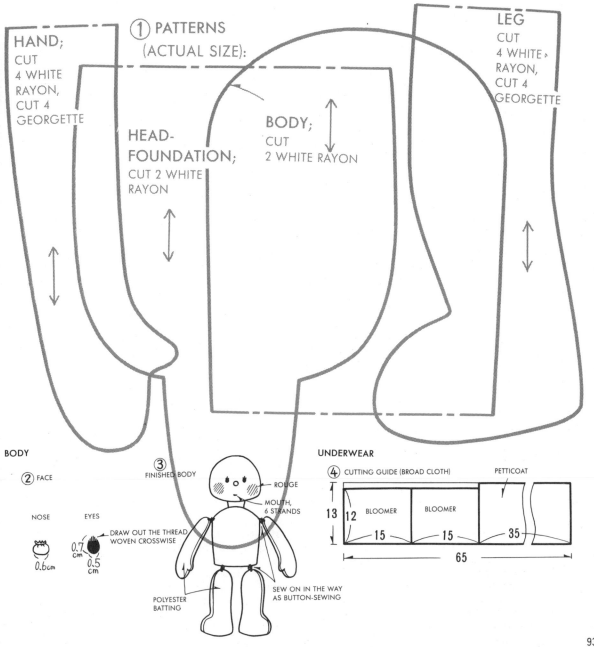

HAND;
CUT
4 WHITE
RAYON,
CUT 4
GEORGETTE

① PATTERNS
(ACTUAL SIZE):

LEG
CUT
4 WHITE
RAYON,
CUT 4
GEORGETTE

HEAD-
FOUNDATION;
CUT 2 WHITE
RAYON

BODY;
CUT
2 WHITE RAYON

BODY

② FACE

③ FINISHED BODY

NOSE   EYES

0.6cm   0.7 cm   0.5 cm

DRAW OUT THE THREAD
WOVEN CROSSWISE

ROUGE

MOUTH,
6 STRANDS

SEW ON IN THE WAY
AS BUTTON-SEWING

POLYESTER
BATTING

UNDERWEAR

④ CUTTING GUIDE (BROAD CLOTH)

PETTICOAT

13 12   BLOOMER   BLOOMER

15   15   35

65

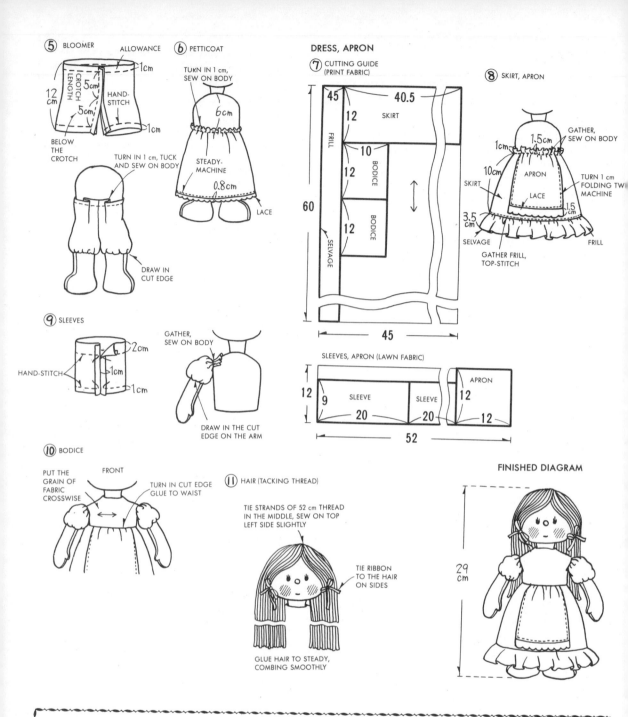

⑤ BLOOMER
ALLOWANCE
1cm
CROTCH LENGTH
12 cm
5cm
5cm
HAND-STITCH
BELOW THE CROTCH
1cm
TURN IN 1 cm, TUCK AND SEW ON BODY
DRAW IN CUT EDGE

⑥ PETTICOAT
TURN IN 1 cm, SEW ON BODY
6cm
STEADY-MACHINE
0.8cm
LACE

DRESS, APRON
⑦ CUTTING GUIDE (PRINT FABRIC)
45
40.5
12
SKIRT
FRILL
10
12
BODICE
12
BODICE
60
SELVAGE
45

⑧ SKIRT, APRON
1.5cm
GATHER, SEW ON BODY
1cm
10cm
SKIRT
APRON
LACE
TURN 1 cm FOLDING TW MACHINE
1.5 cm
3.5 cm
SELVAGE
GATHER FRILL, TOP-STITCH
FRILL

⑨ SLEEVES
2cm
HAND-STITCH
1cm
1cm
GATHER, SEW ON BODY
DRAW IN THE CUT EDGE ON THE ARM

SLEEVES, APRON (LAWN FABRIC)
12
9
SLEEVE
20
SLEEVE
20
APRON
12
12
52

⑩ BODICE
PUT THE GRAIN OF FABRIC CROSSWISE
FRONT
TURN IN CUT EDGE GLUE TO WAIST

⑪ HAIR (TACKING THREAD)
TIE STRANDS OF 52 cm THREAD IN THE MIDDLE, SEW ON TOP LEFT SIDE SLIGHTLY
TIE RIBBON TO THE HAIR ON SIDES
GLUE HAIR TO STEADY, COMBING SMOOTHLY

FINISHED DIAGRAM
29 cm

ELENNE

Shown on page 13.

The hair is colored with black tea. She is ready to sleep in her negligge, so use soft and fancy fabric to express her quiet time.

YOU'LL NEED:
Head-Foundation, Body, Hands, Legs—70 cm by 45 cm White rayon. Face, Nose, Hands, Legs—60 cm by 30 cm Beige georgette. Eyes—Dacron georgette. Mouth—Stranded embroidery thread. Hair—3 skeins of tacking thread. Nightcap, Negligge, Bloomer—90 cm by 60 cm cotton print. 340 cm of 2.5 cm lace. 35 cm of 0.5 cm ribbon. Slipper—30 cm by 12 cm felt. And Others—Packing. Cotton wadding. Polyester

batting.
FINSIHED SIZE: Refer to diagram.
MAKING INSTRUCTIONS:
The basic manner is same as for Hiji, so make referring to page 50–64.
Make feet putting cardboard on soles in same manner as for Hiji, sew on instep and soles of slipper.
Put on negligge after the skirt is stitched to the body.
Sew on hair as shown on page 72, overlay nightcap

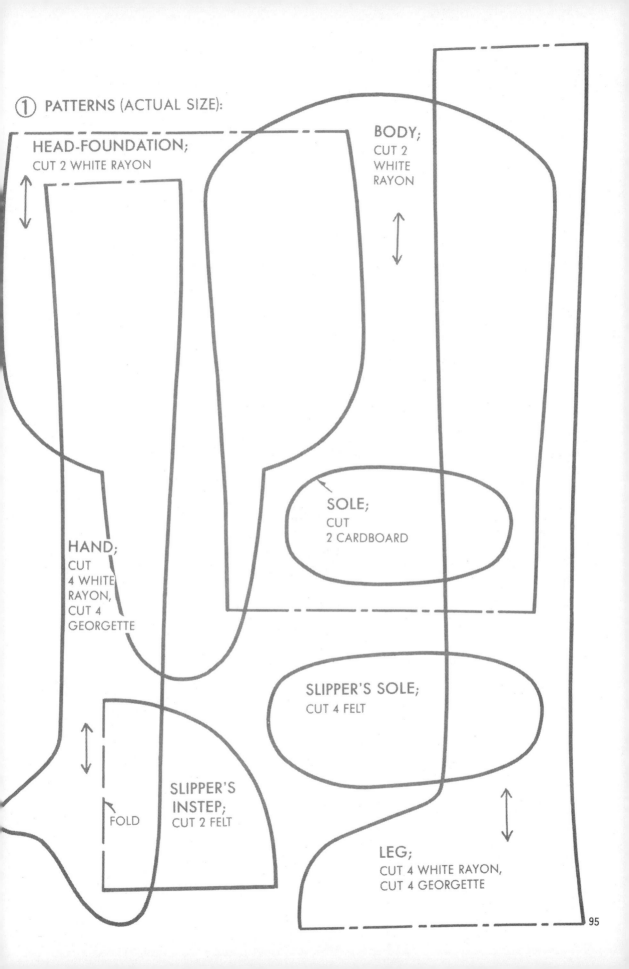

① PATTERNS (ACTUAL SIZE):

HEAD-FOUNDATION;
CUT 2 WHITE RAYON

BODY;
CUT 2
WHITE
RAYON

HAND;
CUT
4 WHITE
RAYON,
CUT 4
GEORGETTE

SOLE;
CUT
2 CARDBOARD

SLIPPER'S SOLE;
CUT 4 FELT

SLIPPER'S
INSTEP;
CUT 2 FELT

FOLD

LEG;
CUT 4 WHITE RAYON,
CUT 4 GEORGETTE

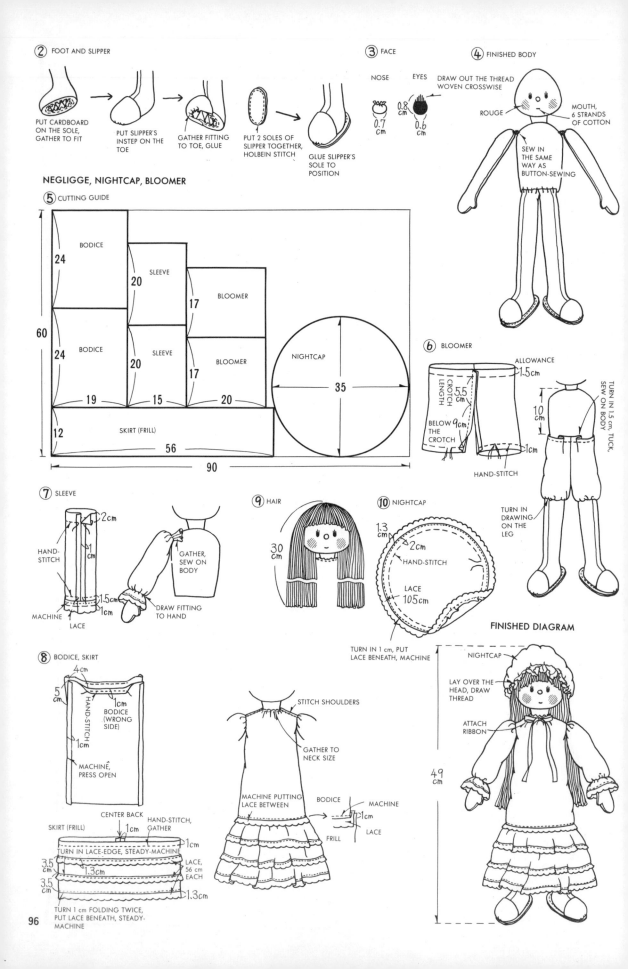

(2) FOOT AND SLIPPER

PUT CARDBOARD ON THE SOLE, GATHER TO FIT

PUT SLIPPER'S INSTEP ON THE TOE

GATHER FITTING TO TOE, GLUE

PUT 2 SOLES OF SLIPPER TOGETHER, HOLBEIN STITCH

GLUE SLIPPER'S SOLE TO POSITION

(3) FACE

NOSE
0.7 cm

EYES
0.8 cm
0.6 cm

(4) FINISHED BODY

DRAW OUT THE THREAD WOVEN CROSSWISE

ROUGE

MOUTH, 6 STRANDS OF COTTON

SEW IN THE SAME WAY AS BUTTON-SEWING

NEGLIGGE, NIGHTCAP, BLOOMER

(5) CUTTING GUIDE

BODICE 24
SLEEVE 20
BLOOMER 17
BODICE 24
SLEEVE 20
BLOOMER 17
60
19 15 20
NIGHTCAP 35
12 SKIRT (FRILL) 56
90

(6) BLOOMER

ALLOWANCE 1.5 cm
CROTCH LENGTH 5.5 cm
BELOW THE CROTCH 9 cm
HAND-STITCH

TURN IN 1.5 cm, TUCK, SEW ON BODY
10 cm
1 cm

TURN IN DRAWING ON THE LEG

(7) SLEEVE

2 cm
1 cm
HAND-STITCH
MACHINE
LACE
1.5 cm
1 cm
GATHER, SEW ON BODY
DRAW FITTING TO HAND

(9) HAIR

30 cm

(10) NIGHTCAP

1.3 cm
2 cm
HAND-STITCH
LACE 105 cm

FINISHED DIAGRAM

(8) BODICE, SKIRT

4 cm
5 cm
HAND-STITCH
1 cm
BODICE (WRONG SIDE)
1 cm
MACHINE, PRESS OPEN

STITCH SHOULDERS
GATHER TO NECK SIZE
TURN IN 1 cm, PUT LACE BENEATH, MACHINE
MACHINE PUTTING LACE BETWEEN
BODICE
MACHINE
1 cm
FRILL
LACE

CENTER BACK
SKIRT (FRILL)
1 cm
HAND-STITCH, GATHER
1 cm
TURN IN LACE-EDGE, STEADY-MACHINE
3.5 cm
1.3 cm
LACE, 56 cm EACH
3.5 cm
1.3 cm
TURN 1 cm FOLDING TWICE, PUT LACE BENEATH, STEADY-MACHINE

NIGHTCAP
LAY OVER THE HEAD, DRAW THREAD
ATTACH RIBBON
49 cm

MAYU

Shown on page 14.

Shown on page 14.

Use new-born baby's socks available in town. Since top of hands and legs has to be stuffed thicker than the opening area, use polyester batting instead of wadding.

YOU'LL NEED:
Head-Foundation, Body, Hands, Legs—90 cm by 65 cm White rayon. Face, Nose, Hands, Legs—90 cm by 50 cm Beige georgette. Eyes—Dacron georgette. Mouth—Stranded embroidery thread. Hair—Sport weight yarn. 60 cm of 0.6 cm ribbon. Bloomer, Dress —90 cm by 30 cm cotton print. 18 cm by 14 cm broad cloth. 70 cm of 3 cm lace. 1.5 cm diameter button. And Others—New-born baby's socks. Packing. Cotton wadding. Polyester batting.

FINISHED SIZE: Refer to diagram.
MAKING INSTRUCTIONS:
The basic manner is same as for Hiji, so make referring to page 50–64.
Legs are finished in the same way as hand, stuffing polyeaster batting. Sew on front bodice after lace is stitched to the york.
Sew on hair same as Hiji, braid on sides, secure the end making a loop with it.

HEAD-FOUNDATION
CUT 2 WHITE RAYON

HAND;
CUT 4
WHITE
RAYON,
CUT 4
GEORGETTE

① PATTERNS (ACTUAL SIZE)

FRONT YOKE;
CUT 1 CENTER
FOLDED BROAD
CLOTH

BODY;
CUT 2
WHITE
RAYON

FOLD

LEG;
CUT 4 WHITE RAYON,
CUT 4 GEORGETTE

FRONT
BODICE;
CUT 1
CENTER
FOLDED
PRINT FABRIC

COLLAR;
CUT 2 CENTER
FOLDED BROAD
CLOTH

FOLD

FOLD

FOLD

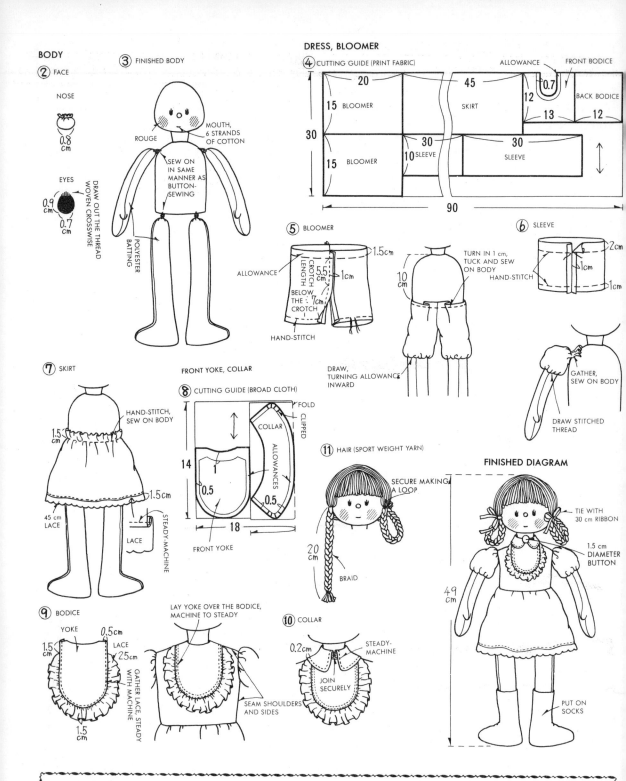

SHIGERU & CHIKO

Shown on page 15.

Use new-born baby's socks. Sweater and muffler are paired to express a modern young couple. Clothe making their heads tilt a little.

YOU'LL NEED (body materials are common):
Head-Foundation, Body, Hands, Legs—73 cm by 48 cm White rayon. Face, Nose, Hands, Legs—63 cm by 48 cm Beige cotton jersey. Eyes—Dacron georgette.

Mouth—Stranded embroidery thread. Hair—Sport weight yarn. 40 cm of 0.6 cm ribbon. And Others—New-born baby's socks. Packing. Cotton wadding. Polyester batting.

(Shigeru): Sweater—Light weight yarn. Pants—36 cm by 12 cm wool fabric.

(Chiko): Blouse—70 cm by 16 cm White jersey. 23 cm of 1 cm braid. Bloomer—36 cm by 12 cm White rayon. Jumper-Skirt—20 cm by 23.5 cm felt. Stranded embroidery cotton. 2 of 1.5 cm diameter button.

FINISHED SIZE: Refer to diagram.

MAKING INSTRUCTIONS:

The basic manner is same as for Hiji, so make referring to page 50–64.

(Shigeru): Make head beforehand, set in position making a hole on the body after sweater is clothed. Sew on hair as shown on page 72.

(Chiko): Make body in the same way as for Shigeru. Part the yarn for hair in half, sew on in same manner as for Hiji as shown. Knit muffler, wrap round the neck.

① PATTERNS (ACTUAL SIZE):

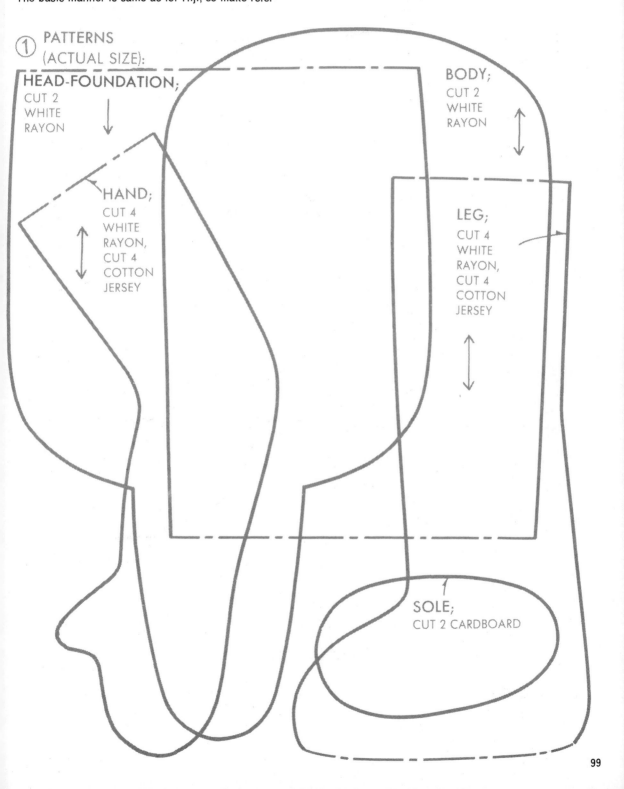

HEAD-FOUNDATION;
CUT 2
WHITE
RAYON

HAND;
CUT 4
WHITE
RAYON,
CUT 4
COTTON
JERSEY

BODY;
CUT 2
WHITE
RAYON

LEG;
CUT 4
WHITE
RAYON,
CUT 4
COTTON
JERSEY

SOLE;
CUT 2 CARDBOARD

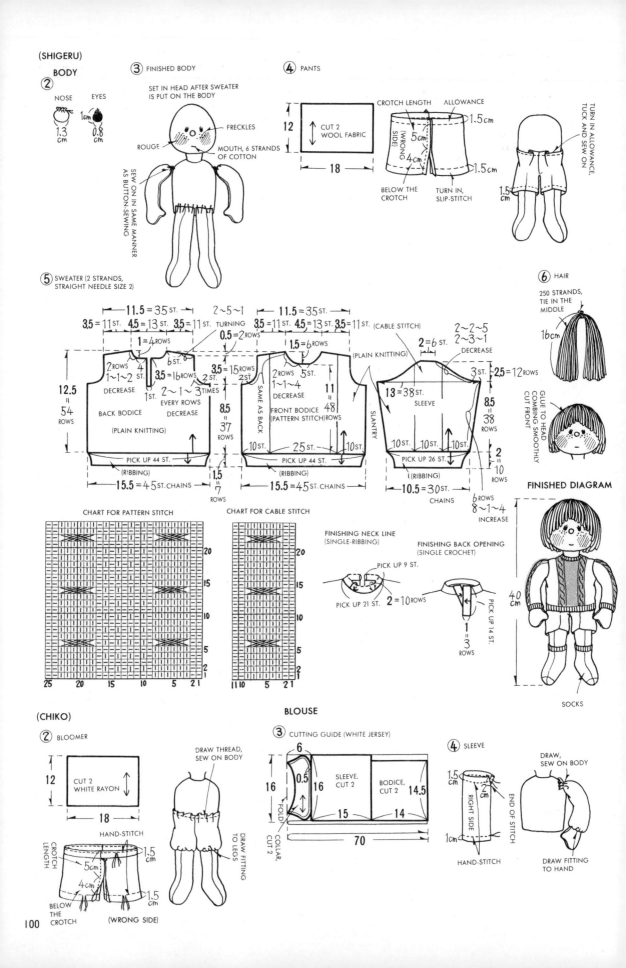

(SHIGERU)

BODY ②

NOSE EYES
1.3 cm 0.8 cm

③ FINISHED BODY

SET IN HEAD AFTER SWEATER IS PUT ON THE BODY

FRECKLES
ROUGE
MOUTH, 6 STRANDS OF COTTON
SEW ON IN SAME MANNER AS BUTTON-SEWING

④ PANTS

12
CUT 2
WOOL FABRIC
18

CROTCH LENGTH ALLOWANCE
(WRONG SIDE) 5cm 4cm 1.5cm
BELOW THE CROTCH TURN IN, SLIP-STITCH 1.5cm

TURN IN ALLOWANCE, TUCK AND SEW ON
1.5 cm

⑤ SWEATER (2 STRANDS, STRAIGHT NEEDLE SIZE 2)

11.5 = 35 ST.   2~5~1   11.5 = 35 ST.
3.5 = 11 ST. 4.5 = 13 ST. 3.5 = 11 ST. TURNING   3.5 = 11 ST. 4.5 = 13 ST. 3.5 = 11 ST. (CABLE STITCH)   2~2~5 2~3~1 DECREASE
0.5 = 2 ROWS
1 = 4 ROWS   1.5 = 6 ROWS   2 = 6 ST.
2 ROWS 4 ST. 6 ST.   6 ST.   (PLAIN KNITTING)   3 ST. 2.5 = 12 ROWS
1~1~2 3.5 = 16 ROWS 2 ST.   2 ROWS 5 ST.   13 = 38 ST. SLEEVE
12.5 = 54 ROWS DECREASE 1 ST. 2~1~3 TIMES 3.5 = 15 ROWS 2 ST.   1~1~4 DECREASE   11 48 ROWS   8.5 = 38 ROWS
BACK BODICE EVERY ROWS DECREASE 8.5 = 37 ROWS   SAME AS BACK FRONT BODICE (PATTERN STITCH)   SLANTRY   10 ST. 10 ST. 10 ST.
(PLAIN KNITTING)   PICK UP 44 ST.   PICK UP 44 ST.   PICK UP 26 ST.   2 = 10 ROWS
(RIBBING)   (RIBBING)   (RIBBING)
15.5 = 45 ST. CHAINS 1.5 = 7 ROWS 15.5 = 45 ST. CHAINS   10.5 = 30 ST. CHAINS   6 ROWS 8~1~4 INCREASE

⑥ HAIR

250 STRANDS, TIE IN THE MIDDLE
16cm

GLUE TO HEAD COMBING SMOOTHLY CUT FRONT

CHART FOR PATTERN STITCH

CHART FOR CABLE STITCH

FINISHING NECK LINE (SINGLE-RIBBING)
PICK UP 9 ST.
PICK UP 21 ST. 2 = 10 ROWS

FINISHING BACK OPENING (SINGLE CROCHET)
PICK UP 14 ST.
1 3 ROWS

FINISHED DIAGRAM
40 cm
SOCKS

(CHIKO)

② BLOOMER

12
CUT 2
WHITE RAYON
18

CROTCH LENGTH 5cm 4cm 1.5cm
BELOW THE CROTCH (WRONG SIDE) 1.5 cm

DRAW THREAD, SEW ON BODY
HAND-STITCH
DRAW FITTING TO LEGS

BLOUSE

③ CUTTING GUIDE (WHITE JERSEY)

6
16 0.5 16   SLEEVE, CUT 2   BODICE, CUT 2 14.5
FOLD COLLAR, CUT 2   15   14
70

④ SLEEVE

1.5 cm 2 cm
RIGHT SIDE END OF STITCH
1cm
HAND-STITCH

DRAW, SEW ON BODY
DRAW FITTING TO HAND

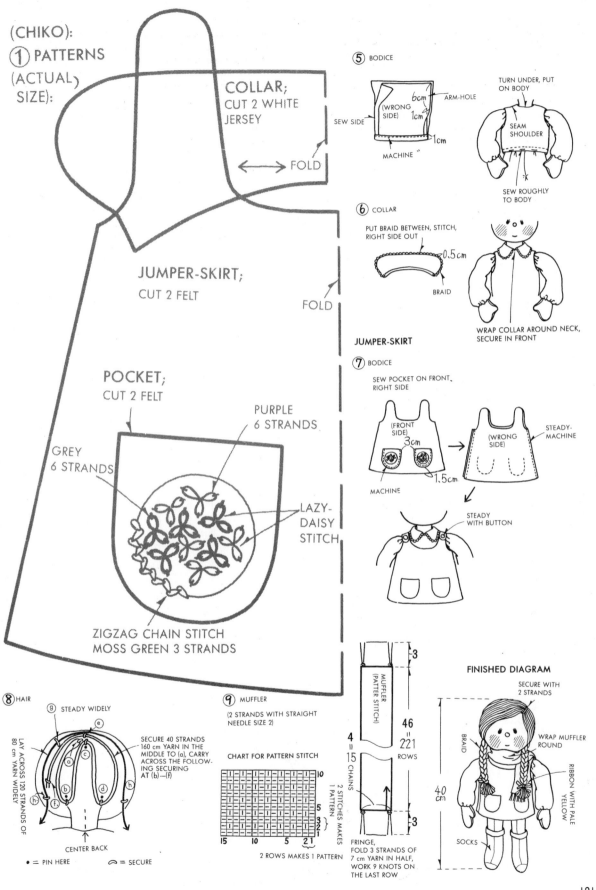

AKKO & GOROH & KENTA

Shown on page 16–17.

Stain clothes putting grey powder-eye-shadow on them. The three are from same pattern, and the clothes for boys are made in the same way. Feature mischievous faces.

YOU'LL NEED (Body materials are common): Head-Foundation, Bady, Hands, Legs—70 cm by 38 cm White rayon. Face, Nos Hands, Legs—55 cm by 25 cm cotton jersey. Eyes—Dacron georgette. Mouth —Stranded embroidery thread. Hair—Light weight yarn. 40 cm of 0.6 cm ribbon. And Others—Packing. Cotton wadding. Polyester batting.
(Akko): Dress, Bloomer—58 cm by 29 cm cotton print. Adhesive plaster—White cotton fabric.
(Goroh): Shirt—50 cm by 14 cm cotton print. Salopette—56 cm by 18 cm light weight denim. Stranded embroidery cotton.

(Kenta): Shirt—50 cm by 14 cm striped cotton. Salopette—56 cm by 18 cm light weight denim. Stranded embroidery cotton.
FINISHED SIZE: Refer to diagram.
MAKING INSTRUCTIONS:
Make three bodies in the same way, referring to page 50–64 for basic manner.
Akko: Cut out dress and bloomers as shown and put on body. Sew on hair in same manner as for Hiji, braid and ribbon making a loop on side.
Goroh: Cut out shirt and salopette as shown and put on body. Sew on hair referring to page 72.
Kenta: Make in same manner as for Goroh.

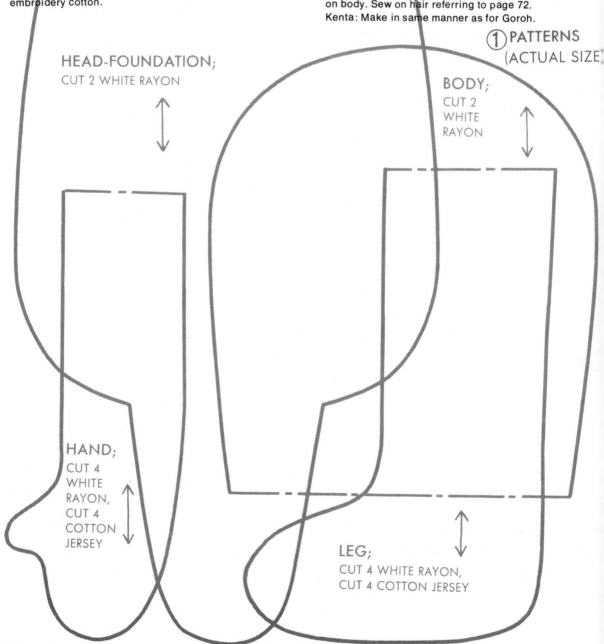

① PATTERNS (ACTUAL SIZE)

HEAD-FOUNDATION;
CUT 2 WHITE RAYON

BODY;
CUT 2
WHITE
RAYON

HAND;
CUT 4
WHITE
RAYON,
CUT 4
COTTON
JERSEY

LEG;
CUT 4 WHITE RAYON,
CUT 4 COTTON JERSEY

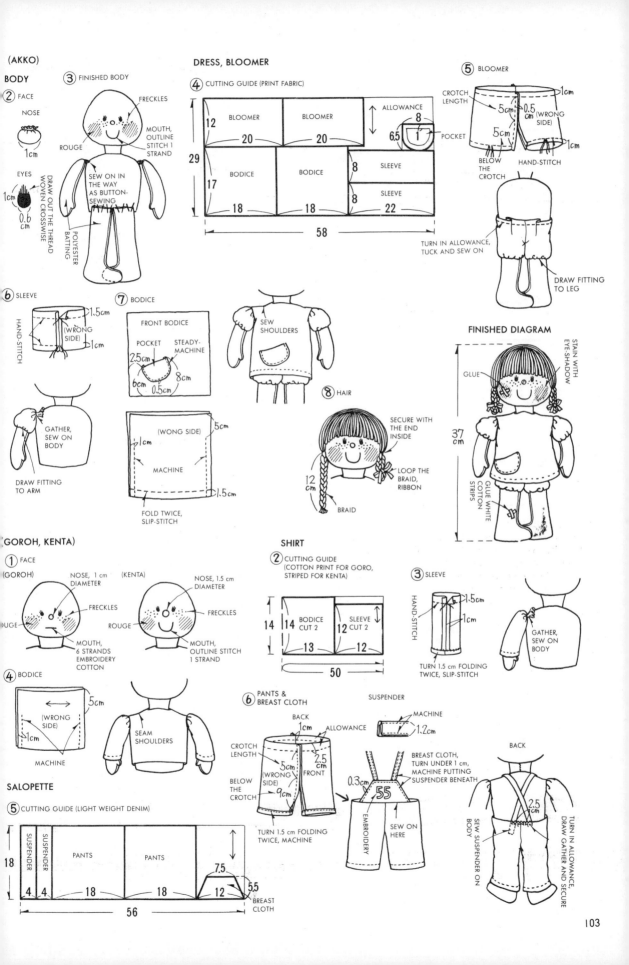

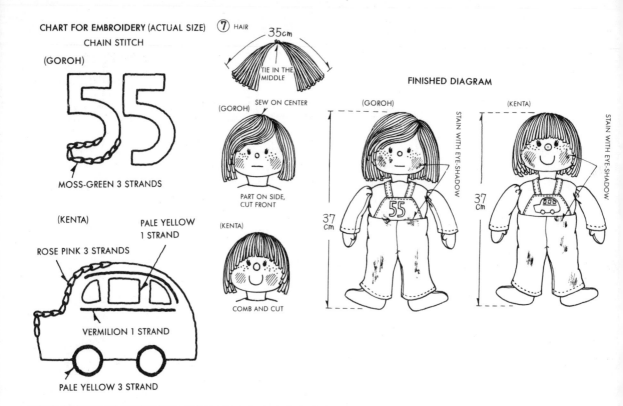

CHART FOR EMBROIDERY (ACTUAL SIZE)
CHAIN STITCH

(GOROH)

55

MOSS-GREEN 3 STRANDS

(KENTA)

ROSE PINK 3 STRANDS

PALE YELLOW 1 STRAND

VERMILION 1 STRAND

PALE YELLOW 3 STRAND

⑦ HAIR

35cm

TIE IN THE MIDDLE

(GOROH)   SEW ON CENTER

PART ON SIDE, CUT FRONT

(KENTA)

COMB AND CUT

FINISHED DIAGRAM

(GOROH)   (KENTA)

STAIN WITH EYE-SHADOW

37 cm

MIDORI & OYUKI

Shown on page 18–19.

Both are made from same pattern. Create hair style combing neatly. Try to use traditional Japanese fabrics.

YOU'LL NEED (for each):
Head-Foundation, Body, Hands, Legs—72 cm by 50 cm White Rayon. Face, Nose, Hands, Legs—60 cm by 50 cm cotton jersey. Eyes—Dacron georgette. Mouth—Stranded embroidery thread. Hair—Sport weight yarn, worsted weight yarn. 14 cm by 15 cm broad cloth. Artificial flower. Kimono—86 cm by 72 cm cotton fabric. Belt—90 cm by 15 cm broad cloth. Collar—8 cm by 25 cm broad cloth. And Others— Packing. Cotton wadding. Polyester batting.
FINISHED SIZE: Refer to diagram.

MAKING INSTRUCTIONS:
The basic manner is same as for Hiji, so make referring to page 50–64.
Sew hands on body, setting in properly.
Sew collar on body, make kimono bodice part and put on body, secure lower half of the front. Make bottom part of the kimono, put on body. Sew belt, put round the waist hiding all the allowances benath, tie on back.
Sew on hair in same manner as for Hiji, bundle as shown, wrap with a fabric piece and secure, putting flowers and decorative belt together.

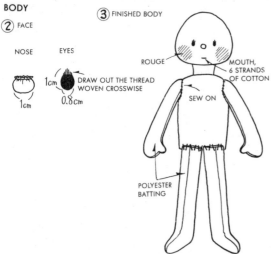

BODY

② FACE

NOSE   EYES

1cm   DRAW OUT THE THREAD WOVEN CROSSWISE
0.8cm

1cm

③ FINISHED BODY

ROUGE

MOUTH, 6 STRANDS OF COTTON

SEW ON

POLYESTER BATTING

KIMONO

④ COLLAR (BROAD CLOTH)

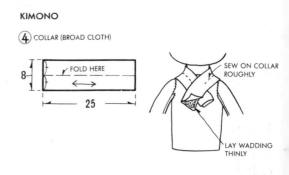

8

FOLD HERE

25

SEW ON COLLAR ROUGHLY

LAY WADDING THINLY

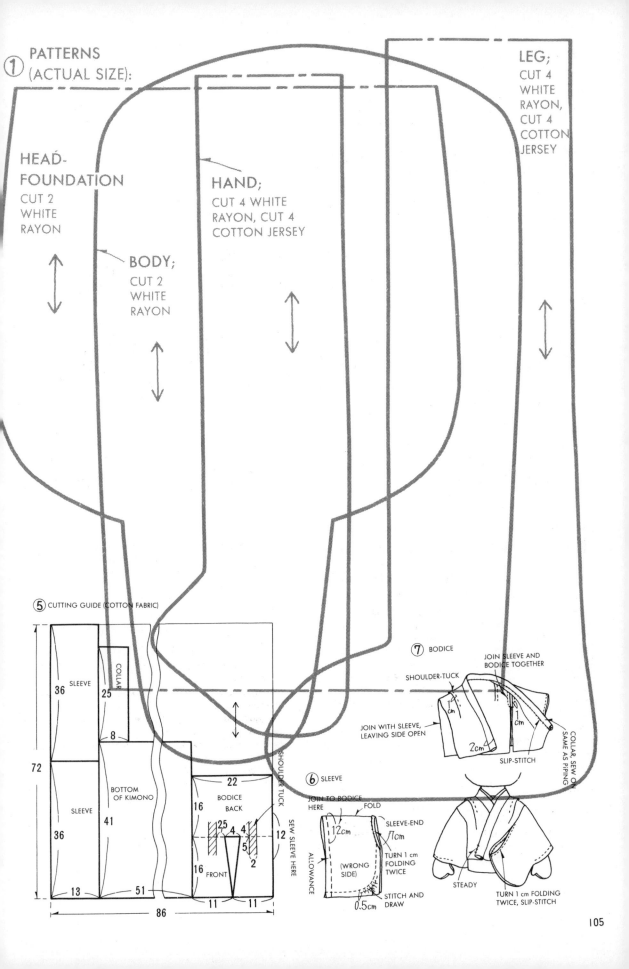

① PATTERNS (ACTUAL SIZE):

LEG;
CUT 4
WHITE
RAYON,
CUT 4
COTTON
JERSEY

HEAD-
FOUNDATION
CUT 2
WHITE
RAYON

HAND;
CUT 4 WHITE
RAYON, CUT 4
COTTON JERSEY

BODY;
CUT 2
WHITE
RAYON

⑤ CUTTING GUIDE (COTTON FABRIC)

SLEEVE   36
COLLAR 25
8

72

SLEEVE   36
BOTTOM OF KIMONO   41

13   51
11   11
86

22
16
BODICE BACK
25   4 4
5
16   FRONT   2
12

SHOULDER TUCK
SEW SLEEVE HERE

⑦ BODICE

SHOULDER-TUCK

JOIN SLEEVE AND
BODICE TOGETHER

JOIN WITH SLEEVE,
LEAVING SIDE OPEN

1cm   1cm
2cm

SLIP-STITCH

COLLAR, SEW ON
SAME AS PIPING

⑥ SLEEVE

JOIN TO BODICE
HERE   FOLD

12cm

(WRONG
SIDE)

ALLOWANCE

SLEEVE-END
1cm

TURN 1 cm
FOLDING
TWICE

STITCH AND
DRAW
0.5cm

STEADY

TURN 1 cm FOLDING
TWICE, SLIP-STITCH

105

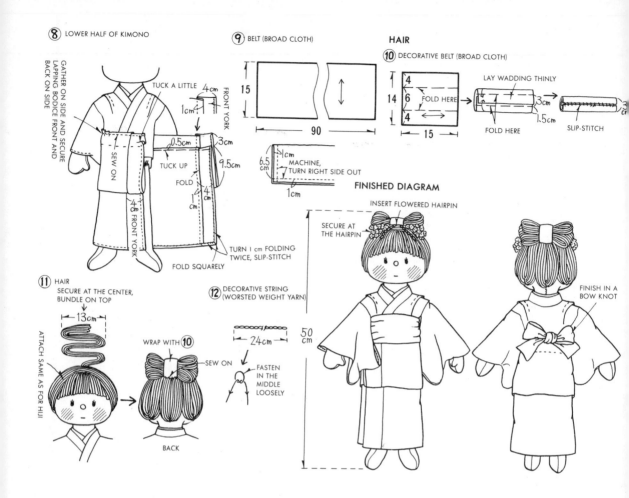

⑧ LOWER HALF OF KIMONO

GATHER ON SIDE AND SECURE LAPPING BODICE FRONT AND BACK ON SIDE

TUCK A LITTLE

4 cm

1 cm

FRONT YORK

SEW ON

0.5 cm

3 cm

TUCK UP

9.5 cm

FOLD

1 4 cm

4 cm FRONT YORK

TURN 1 cm FOLDING TWICE, SLIP-STITCH

FOLD SQUARELY

⑨ BELT (BROAD CLOTH)

15

90

⑩ DECORATIVE BELT (BROAD CLOTH)

4
14 6 FOLD HERE
4

15

LAY WADDING THINLY

FOLD HERE

3 cm

1.5 cm

SLIP-STITCH

1 cm
MACHINE, TURN RIGHT SIDE OUT
6.5
1 cm

HAIR

⑪ HAIR
SECURE AT THE CENTER, BUNDLE ON TOP

13 cm

ATTACH SAME AS FOR HIJI

WRAP WITH ⑩

SEW ON

BACK

⑫ DECORATIVE STRING (WORSTED WEIGHT YARN)

24 cm

FASTEN IN THE MIDDLE LOOSELY

FINISHED DIAGRAM

INSERT FLOWERED HAIRPIN

SECURE AT THE HAIRPIN

50 cm

FINISH IN A BOW KNOT

PRINCE & PRINCESS

Shown on page 20–21.

Put a piece of wire into hands and legs and pose them as you like. Make a stand of board higher than 2.5 cm, then hole with gimlet to set each foot steadily on the board.

YOU'LL NEED (body materials are common):
Head-Foundation, Body, Hands, Legs—50 cm by 30 cm White rayon. Face, Nose, Hands—33 cm by 28 cm Beige georgette. Eyes—Dacron georgette. Mouth—Stranded embroidery thread. Hair—Mohair yarn. And Others—Wire No. 12, No. 18. Packing. Cotton wadding. Polyster batting.
(Prince): Legs—28 cm by 14 cm silver lame. Sleeves—24 cm by 16 cm dacron seersucker. 40 cm of 2 cm lace. Bodice, Hat—44 cm by 13 cm Purple felt. 100 cm of 2.5 cm braid. Shoes—26 cm of 2 cm Black and Gold braid. 5 cm by 4.5 cm Black felt.
(Princess): Legs, Bloomers—28 cm by 26 cm White georgette. 44 cm of 4 cm lace. Petticoat—45 cm by 10 cm non woven fabric. Dress—69 cm by 18 cm White lace. 170 cm of 1.8 cm floral braid. 15 cm of 2 cm lace. Hair Ornament, Bouquet—Artificial flowers, leaves. 10 cm of 1.8 cm floral braid. Shoes—26 cm of 2 cm Pale Pink braid. 5 cm by 4.5 cm White felt.
FINISHED SIZE: Refer to diagram.

MAKING INSTRUCTIONS:
The basic manner is same as for Hiji, so make referring to page 50–64.
Prince: Make hands and legs with the wire inserted right in the middle, set them inbody inserting those of wire into.
Let him stand, inserting the wire out from legs into their stands.
Princess: Make body in same manner as for prince, put on underwear and dress.
Sew on hair in the same way as for Hiji, attach back hair of twined yarns. Sew on hair ornament, let her hold bouquet in the hand bended.

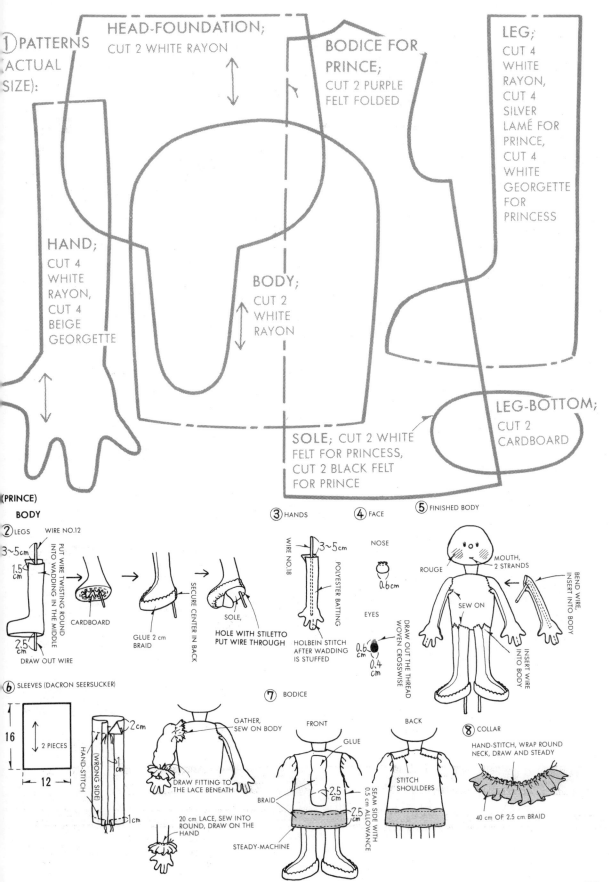

① PATTERNS (ACTUAL SIZE):

HEAD-FOUNDATION; CUT 2 WHITE RAYON

BODICE FOR PRINCE; CUT 2 PURPLE FELT FOLDED

LEG; CUT 4 WHITE RAYON, CUT 4 SILVER LAMÉ FOR PRINCE, CUT 4 WHITE GEORGETTE FOR PRINCESS

HAND; CUT 4 WHITE RAYON, CUT 4 BEIGE GEORGETTE

BODY; CUT 2 WHITE RAYON

SOLE; CUT 2 WHITE FELT FOR PRINCESS, CUT 2 BLACK FELT FOR PRINCE

LEG-BOTTOM; CUT 2 CARDBOARD

(PRINCE)

BODY

② LEGS

WIRE NO.12

3~5cm
1.5 cm
PUT WIRE TWISTING INTO WADDING IN THE MIDDLE
2.5cm
DRAW OUT WIRE

CARDBOARD

SECURE CENTER IN BACK

GLUE 2 cm BRAID

SOLE, HOLE WITH STILETTO PUT WIRE THROUGH

③ HANDS

WIRE NO.18
3~5cm
POLYESTER BATTING
HOLBEIN STITCH AFTER WADDING IS STUFFED

④ FACE

NOSE
0.6cm

EYES
0.6 cm
0.4 cm
DRAW OUT THE THREAD WOVEN CROSSWISE

⑤ FINISHED BODY

ROUGE
MOUTH, 2 STRANDS
BEND WIRE, INSERT INTO BODY
SEW ON
INSERT WIRE INTO BODY

⑥ SLEEVES (DACRON SEERSUCKER)

16
2 PIECES
12
HAND-STITCH
(WRONG SIDE)
2cm
1 cm
1cm

GATHER, SEW ON BODY

DRAW FITTING TO THE LACE BENEATH

20 cm LACE, SEW INTO ROUND, DRAW ON THE HAND

⑦ BODICE

FRONT
GLUE
BRAID
2.5 cm
STEADY-MACHINE

BACK
STITCH SHOULDERS
SEAM SIDE WITH 0.5 cm ALLOWANCE
2.5 cm

⑧ COLLAR

HAND-STITCH, WRAP ROUND NECK, DRAW AND STEADY

40 cm OF 2.5 cm BRAID

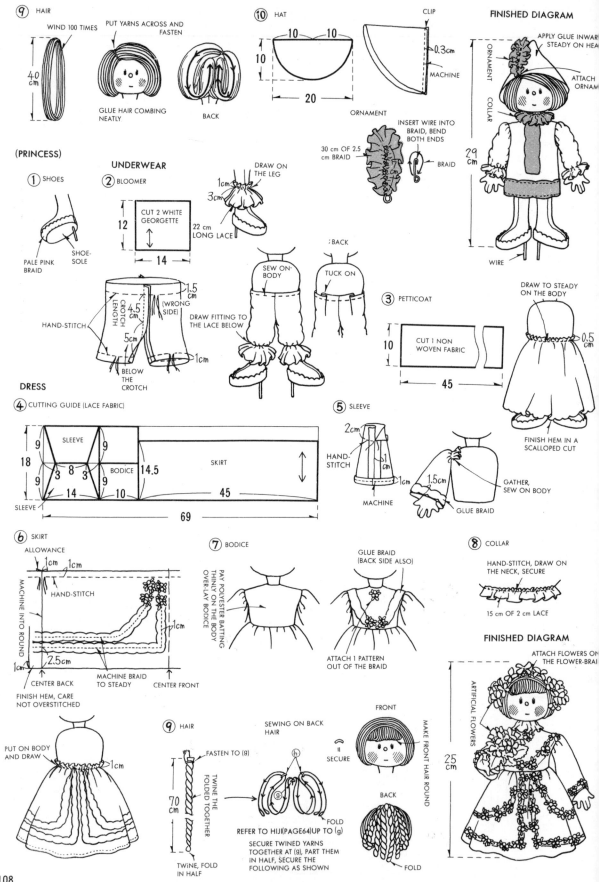

⑨ HAIR

WIND 100 TIMES

40 cm

PUT YARNS ACROSS AND FASTEN

GLUE HAIR COMBING NEATLY

BACK

⑩ HAT

10 10

10

20

CLIP

0.3cm

MACHINE

ORNAMENT

30 cm OF 2.5 cm BRAID

INSERT WIRE INTO BRAID, BEND BOTH ENDS

BRAID

FINISHED DIAGRAM

ORNAMENT   COLLAR

APPLY GLUE INWAR STEADY ON HEA

ATTACH ORN

29 cm

WIRE

(PRINCESS)

UNDERWEAR

① SHOES

PALE PINK BRAID

SHOE-SOLE

② BLOOMER

12

14

CUT 2 WHITE GEORGETTE

22 cm LONG LACE

1cm

3cm

DRAW ON THE LEG

CROTCH LENGTH

4.5 cm

(WRONG SIDE)

1.5 cm

HAND-STITCH

5cm

1cm

BELOW THE CROTCH

SEW ON BODY

BACK

TUCK ON

DRAW FITTING TO THE LACE BELOW

③ PETTICOAT

10

45

CUT 1 NON WOVEN FABRIC

DRAW TO STEADY ON THE BODY

0.5 cm

FINISH HEM IN A SCALLOPED CUT

DRESS

④ CUTTING GUIDE (LACE FABRIC)

9   9

SLEEVE

18   3 8 3   BODICE 14.5

9   9

SLEEVE   14   10

69

SKIRT

45

⑤ SLEEVE

2cm

HAND-STITCH

1 cm

1cm

MACHINE

1.5cm

GATHER, SEW ON BODY

GLUE BRAID

⑥ SKIRT

ALLOWANCE

1cm 1cm

HAND-STITCH

MACHINE INTO ROUND

1cm

2.5cm

MACHINE BRAID TO STEADY

CENTER BACK

1cm

CENTER FRONT

FINISH HEM, CARE NOT OVERSTITCHED

PUT ON BODY AND DRAW

1cm

⑦ BODICE

PAY POLYESTER BATTING THINLY ON THE BODY OVER-LAY BODICE

GLUE BRAID (BACK SIDE ALSO)

ATTACH 1 PATTERN OUT OF THE BRAID

⑧ COLLAR

HAND-STITCH, DRAW ON THE NECK, SECURE

15 cm OF 2 cm LACE

FINISHED DIAGRAM

ATTACH FLOWERS ON THE FLOWER-BRAI

ARTIFICIAL FLOWERS

25 cm

⑨ HAIR

FASTEN TO (9)

70 cm

TWINE THE FOLDED TOGETHER

TWINE, FOLD IN HALF

SEWING ON BACK HAIR

(h)

(9)

SECURE

FOLD

REFER TO HIJI(PAGE64)UP TO (g)

SECURE TWINED YARNS TOGETHER AT (9), PART THEM IN HALF, SECURE THE FOLLOWING AS SHOWN

FRONT

MAKE FRONT HAIR ROUND

BACK

FOLD

LILLIPUTIONS IN THE WOODS

Shown on page 22.

Very simple dolls. Hands and legs are free to move, if strings are tied on them, they would turn to marionettes. Feature their humorous expressions.

YOU'LL NEED (for each):
Head-Foundation, Body, Hands, Legs—40 cm by 30 cm White rayon. Face, Hands—70 cm by 22 cm Beige cotton jersey. Legs—35 cm by 14 cm striped cotton. Nose—Scrap of Orange jersey. Eyes—Dacron georgette. Mouth—Stranded embroidery thread. Hair—Heavy weight yarns. Clothes—30 cm by 29 cm Olive Green felt. 2 of 1.2 cm diameter button. Shoes—16 cm by 8 cm Pale Yellow felt. And Others—Packing. Cotton wadding. Polyester batting.
FINISHED SIZE: Refer to diagram.

MAKING INSTRUCTIONS:
The basic manner is same as for Hiji, so make referring to page 50–64.
Make legs with striped fabric, finish in the same way as hand. Use nose fabric colored with felt point pen. Sew on hair as shown on page 72, finish front hair in a ladder cut.

① PATTERNS (ACTUAL SIZE):

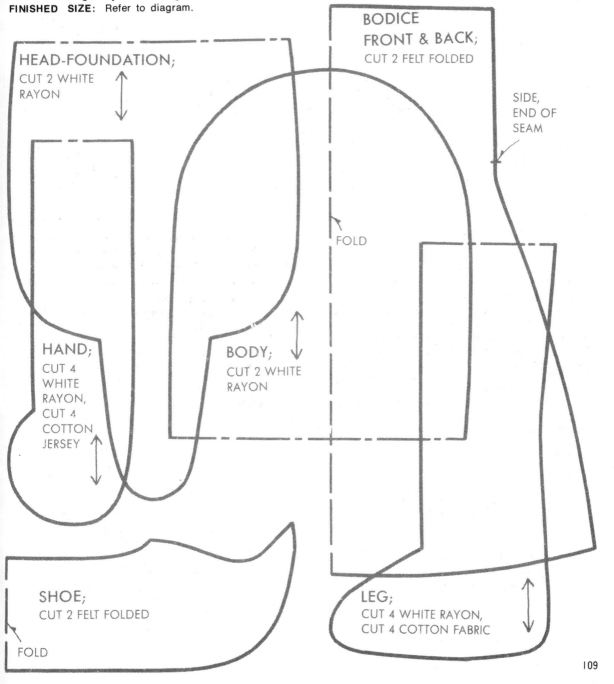

BODICE FRONT & BACK;
CUT 2 FELT FOLDED

SIDE, END OF SEAM

HEAD-FOUNDATION;
CUT 2 WHITE RAYON

FOLD

HAND;
CUT 4 WHITE RAYON,
CUT 4 COTTON JERSEY

BODY;
CUT 2 WHITE RAYON

SHOE;
CUT 2 FELT FOLDED

FOLD

LEG;
CUT 4 WHITE RAYON,
CUT 4 COTTON FABRIC

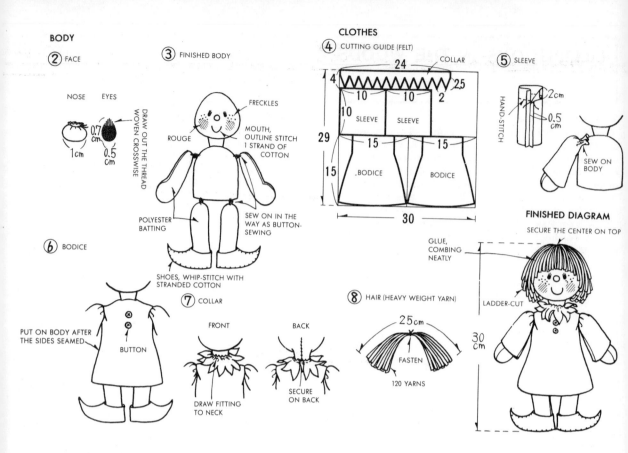

BODY

② FACE

③ FINISHED BODY

NOSE EYES

DRAW OUT THE THREAD WOVEN CROSSWISE

1cm 0.7 cm 0.5 cm

FRECKLES

ROUGE

MOUTH, OUTLINE STITCH 1 STRAND OF COTTON

POLYESTER BATTING

SEW ON IN THE WAY AS BUTTON-SEWING

SHOES, WHIP-STITCH WITH STRANDED COTTON

⑥ BODICE

PUT ON BODY AFTER THE SIDES SEAMED

Ⓐ Ⓑ

BUTTON

CLOTHES

④ CUTTING GUIDE (FELT)

COLLAR

24

4

25

10 10 2

10 SLEEVE SLEEVE

29

15 15

15 BODICE BODICE

30

⑦ COLLAR

FRONT

BACK

DRAW FITTING TO NECK

SECURE ON BACK

⑤ SLEEVE

HAND-STITCH

2cm

0.5 cm

SEW ON BODY

FINISHED DIAGRAM

SECURE THE CENTER ON TOP

GLUE, COMBING NEATLY

LADDER-CUT

30 cm

⑧ HAIR (HEAVY WEIGHT YARN)

25cm

FASTEN

120 YARNS

STRAY ANGELS

Shown on page 23.

Hands and legs are finished with the wire inside, so make them pose as you like. The hair ornament used here is a braid of flowers you may create.

YOU'LL NEED (for each):
Head-Foundation, Body, Hands, Legs—48 cm by 30 cm White rayon. Face, Nose, Hands, Legs—64 cm by 16 cm cotton jersey. Eyes—Dacron georgette. Mouth—Stranded embroidery thread. Hair—Light weight yarn. 20 cm of 1.2 cm floral braid. Clothes—46 cm by 10.5 cm wool georgette. Wings—13 cm by 6.5 cm White lace fabric, non fabric iron-on interfacing. And Others—No. 18 wire. Packing. Cotton wadding. Polyester batting.
FINISHED SIZE: Refer to diagram.

MAKING INSTRUCTIONS:
The basic manner is same as for Hiji, so make referring to page 50–64.
Stuff polyester batting into hands and legs top parts only, insert the wire wrapped with wadding into right in the middle. Sew on legs in a sitting form.
Attach the wings of lace fabric pressed on non woven fabric on back.
Bend hands to make them pose.

BODY

② HANDS, LEGS

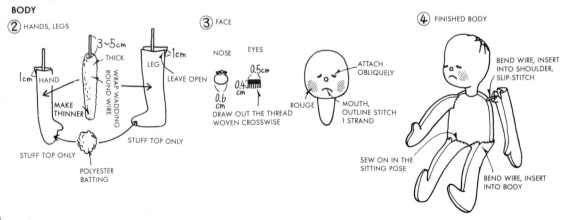

3~5cm

THICK

1cm HAND

LEG

1cm

LEAVE OPEN

MAKE THINNER

WRAP WADDING ROUND WIRE

STUFF TOP ONLY

STUFF TOP ONLY

STUFF TOP ONLY

POLYESTER BATTING

③ FACE

NOSE EYES

0.5cm

0.4 cm

0.6 cm

DRAW OUT THE THREAD WOVEN CROSSWISE

ROUGE

MOUTH, OUTLINE STITCH 1 STRAND

ATTACH OBLIQUELY

④ FINISHED BODY

BEND WIRE, INSERT INTO SHOULDER, SLIP-STITCH

SEW ON IN THE SITTING POSE

BEND WIRE, INSERT INTO BODY

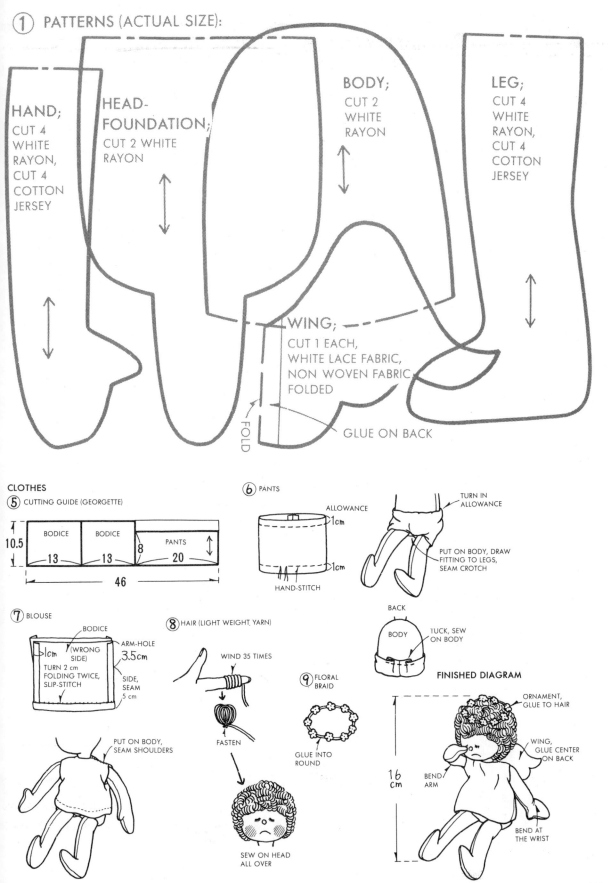

① PATTERNS (ACTUAL SIZE):

HAND;
CUT 4
WHITE
RAYON,
CUT 4
COTTON
JERSEY

HEAD-
FOUNDATION;
CUT 2 WHITE
RAYON

BODY;
CUT 2
WHITE
RAYON

LEG;
CUT 4
WHITE
RAYON,
CUT 4
COTTON
JERSEY

WING;
CUT 1 EACH,
WHITE LACE FABRIC,
NON WOVEN FABRIC,
FOLDED

FOLD

GLUE ON BACK

CLOTHES

⑤ CUTTING GUIDE (GEORGETTE)

	BODICE	BODICE		PANTS
10.5	13	13	8	20

46

⑥ PANTS

ALLOWANCE
1cm

1cm

HAND-STITCH

TURN IN
ALLOWANCE

PUT ON BODY, DRAW
FITTING TO LEGS,
SEAM CROTCH

⑦ BLOUSE

BODICE
(WRONG
SIDE)
1cm
TURN 2 cm
FOLDING TWICE,
SLIP-STITCH

ARM-HOLE
3.5cm

SIDE,
SEAM
5 cm

PUT ON BODY,
SEAM SHOULDERS

⑧ HAIR (LIGHT WEIGHT, YARN)

WIND 35 TIMES

FASTEN

SEW ON HEAD
ALL OVER

⑨ FLORAL
BRAID

GLUE INTO
ROUND

BACK

BODY

TUCK, SEW
ON BODY

FINISHED DIAGRAM

ORNAMENT,
GLUE TO HAIR

WING,
GLUE CENTER
ON BACK

BEND
ARM

BEND AT
THE WRIST

16
cm

111

FANTASY

Shown on page 24–25.

Those are posed dolls, clothed in felt. Make silver flute, wrapping tin foil over a piece of wire. Use same pattern for all fairies. Feature the girl's lovely mood.

YOU'LL NEED:

(Each Boy): Head-Foundation, Body—40 cm by 13 cm White rayon. Face, Nose—12 cm by 14 cm cotton jersey. Hands, Legs—48 cm by 12 cm striped cotton. Eyes—Dacron georgette. Mouth—Stranded embroidery thread. Hair—Mohair yarn. Clothes—38 cm by 12.5 cm Green felt. 20 cm of 1.3 cm braid. And Others—No. 18 wire. Packing. Cotton wadding. Polyester batting.

(Girl): Head-Foundation, Body, Hands, Legs—88 cm by 13 cm White rayon. Face, Nose, Hands, Legs—60 cm by 14 cm cotton jersey. Eyes—Dacron georgette. Mouth—Stranded embroidery thread. Hair—Mohair yarn. 34 cm of 1.8 cm floral braid. Clothes—20 cm by 12.5 cm Pale Yellow felt. 20 cm of 1.8 cm floral braid. Flute—10 cm of No. 16 wire. Tin foil. And Others—No. 18 wire. Packing. Cotton wadding. Polyester batting.

FINISHED SIZE: Refer to diagram.
MAKING INSTRUCTIONS:

The basic manner is same as for Hiji, so make referring to page 50–64.

Boys: Make hands and legs with cotton fabric. As for the way to stuff hands and legs and the way to set up bodies, refere to page 110. Sew on hair as shown on page 72.

Pose them, bending their hands and iegs.

Girl: Make in same manner as for bodys. Feature face, secure flute on her hands inward.

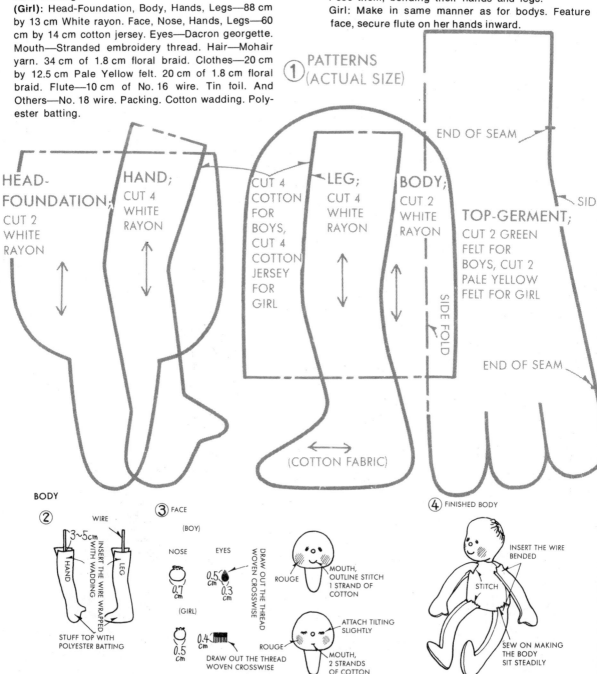

① PATTERNS (ACTUAL SIZE)

HEAD-FOUNDATION; CUT 2 WHITE RAYON

HAND; CUT 4 WHITE RAYON

CUT 4 COTTON FOR BOYS, CUT 4 COTTON JERSEY FOR GIRL

LEG; CUT 4 WHITE RAYON

(COTTON FABRIC)

BODY; CUT 2 WHITE RAYON

SIDE FOLD

END OF SEAM

SIDE

TOP-GERMENT; CUT 2 GREEN FELT FOR BOYS, CUT 2 PALE YELLOW FELT FOR GIRL

END OF SEAM

BODY

② 3~5cm
WIRE
HAND
LEG
INSERT THE WIRE WRAPPED WITH WADDING
STUFF TOP WITH POLYESTER BATTING

③ FACE
(BOY)
NOSE
0.7 cm
EYES
0.5 cm   0.3 cm
DRAW OUT THE THREAD WOVEN CROSSWISE
ROUGE
MOUTH, OUTLINE STITCH 1 STRAND OF COTTON

(GIRL)
0.5 cm
0.4 cm
DRAW OUT THE THREAD WOVEN CROSSWISE
ROUGE
ATTACH TILTING SLIGHTLY
MOUTH, 2 STRANDS OF COTTON

④ FINISHED BODY
INSERT THE WIRE BENDED
STITCH
SEW ON MAKING THE BODY SIT STEADILY

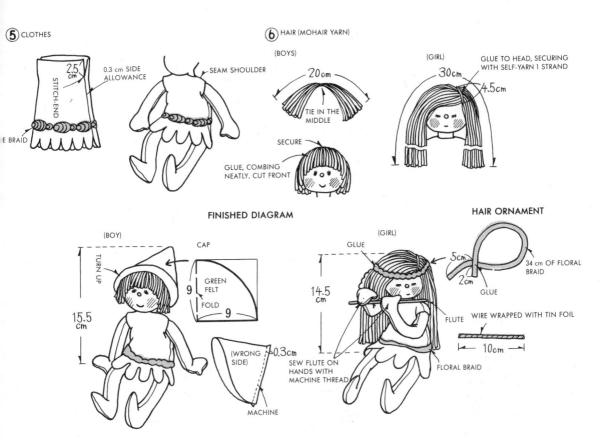

⑤ CLOTHES

2.5 cm

0.3 cm SIDE ALLOWANCE

STITCH-END

E BRAID

SEAM SHOULDER

⑥ HAIR (MOHAIR YARN)

(BOYS)

20 cm

TIE IN THE MIDDLE

SECURE

GLUE, COMBING NEATLY, CUT FRONT

(GIRL)

30 cm

4.5 cm

GLUE TO HEAD, SECURING WITH SELF-YARN 1 STRAND

FINISHED DIAGRAM

HAIR ORNAMENT

(BOY)

TURN UP

15.5 cm

CAP

9

GREEN FELT

FOLD

9

(WRONG SIDE)

0.3 cm

MACHINE

(GIRL)

GLUE

14.5 cm

FLUTE

SEW FLUTE ON HANDS WITH MACHINE THREAD

FLORAL BRAID

5 cm

2 cm

GLUE

34 cm OF FLORAL BRAID

WIRE WRAPPED WITH TIN FOIL

10 cm

THE LAND OF PRE-BIRTH BABIES

Shown on page 26–27.

Make them using same pattern, and put variations on their posing. Finish packing neatly, for bodies are used as they are. Feature their baby like poses.

YOU'LL NEED (for each):
Head-Foundation, Body, Hands, Legs—37.5 cm by 17 cm White rayon. Face, Nose, Body, Hands, Legs —28.5 cm by 17 cm cotton jersey. Eyes—Dacron georgette. Hair—Light weight yarn. Swaddle—16 cm by 10 cm georgette. And Others—No. 18 wire. Packing. Cotton wadding. Polyester batting.
FINISHED SIZE: Refer to diagram.

MAKING INSTRUCTIONS:
The basic manner is same as for Hiji, so make referring to page 50–64.
Sew body in the same way as hands and legs, stuff packing.
Stuff hands and legs referring to page 110, sew on head, hands, legs forming their poses.
Sew on hair as shown on page 72. Pose them bending hands and legs as you see in the picture.

① **PATTERNS** (ACTUAL SIZE):

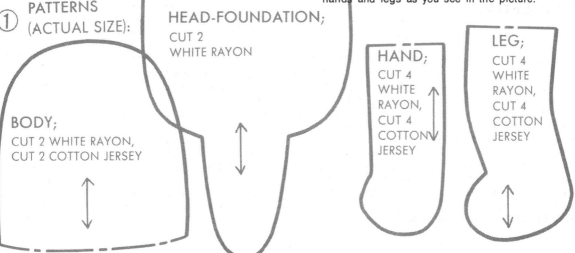

HEAD-FOUNDATION;
CUT 2
WHITE RAYON

BODY;
CUT 2 WHITE RAYON,
CUT 2 COTTON JERSEY

HAND;
CUT 4
WHITE
RAYON,
CUT 4
COTTON
JERSEY

LEG;
CUT 4
WHITE
RAYON,
CUT 4
COTTON
JERSEY

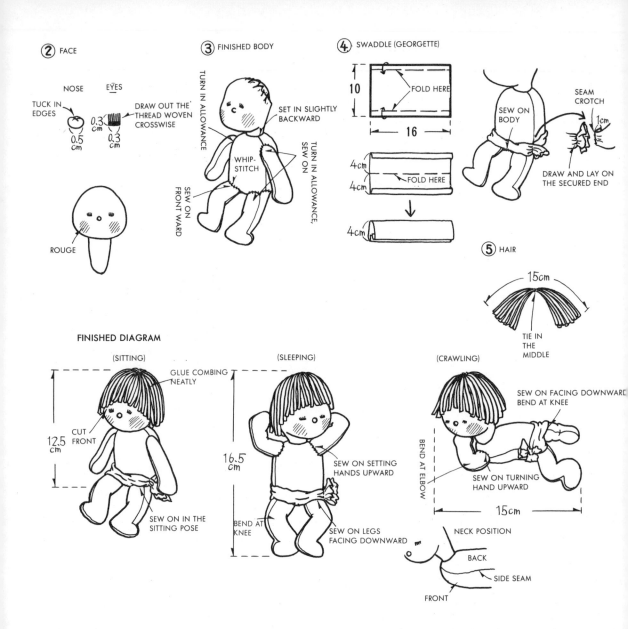

② FACE

NOSE
TUCK IN EDGES
0.5 cm

EYES
0.3 cm   0.3 cm
DRAW OUT THE THREAD WOVEN CROSSWISE

ROUGE

③ FINISHED BODY

TURN IN ALLOWANCE
SET IN SLIGHTLY BACKWARD
WHIP-STITCH
TURN IN ALLOWANCE, SEW ON
SEW ON FRONT WARD

④ SWADDLE (GEORGETTE)

10   16
FOLD HERE

4cm   4cm
FOLD HERE

4cm

SEW ON BODY
SEAM CROTCH
1cm
DRAW AND LAY ON THE SECURED END

⑤ HAIR

15cm
TIE IN THE MIDDLE

FINISHED DIAGRAM

(SITTING)
12.5 cm
GLUE COMBING NEATLY
CUT FRONT
SEW ON IN THE SITTING POSE

(SLEEPING)
16.5 cm
SEW ON SETTING HANDS UPWARD
BEND AT KNEE
SEW ON LEGS FACING DOWNWARD

(CRAWLING)
SEW ON FACING DOWNWARD BEND AT KNEE
BEND AT ELBOW
SEW ON TURNING HAND UPWARD
15cm

NECK POSITION
BACK
SIDE SEAM
FRONT

ONDEENA

Shown on page 28.

The choice of materials of hair and dress is the key to make her look more nymph like. Try to get the yarn of this kind. Study the balance of hands and legs in posing.

YOU'LL NEED:
Head-Foundation, Body, Hands, Legs—80 cm by 37 cm White rayon. Face, Nose, Body, Hands, legs—80 cm by 40 cm cotton jersey. Body—24 cm by 22 cm White georgette. Eyes—Dacron georgette. Mouth—Stranded embroidery thread. Hair—White lame yarn. Artificial flower. Dress—54 cm by 46 cm White georgette. 17 cm of 1.8 cm braid. Bouquet—Artificial flower. And Others—100 cm of 0.4 cm ribbon. No. 18 wire. Packing. Cotton wadding. Polyester batting. 13 cm of White elastic.
FINISHED SIZE: Refer to diagram.

MAKING INSTRUCTIONS:
The basic manner is same as for Hiji, so make referring to page 50–64.
Make body with White rayon, overlapping cotton jersey and then georgette.
Make hands and legs referring to page 107. Cut out soles, stitch to position.
Put on dress, belt the waist. Bundle a little of hair on right side, glue hair ornament.
Bend hands and legs as shown, sew bouquet on hands, secure legs at the knee to steady.

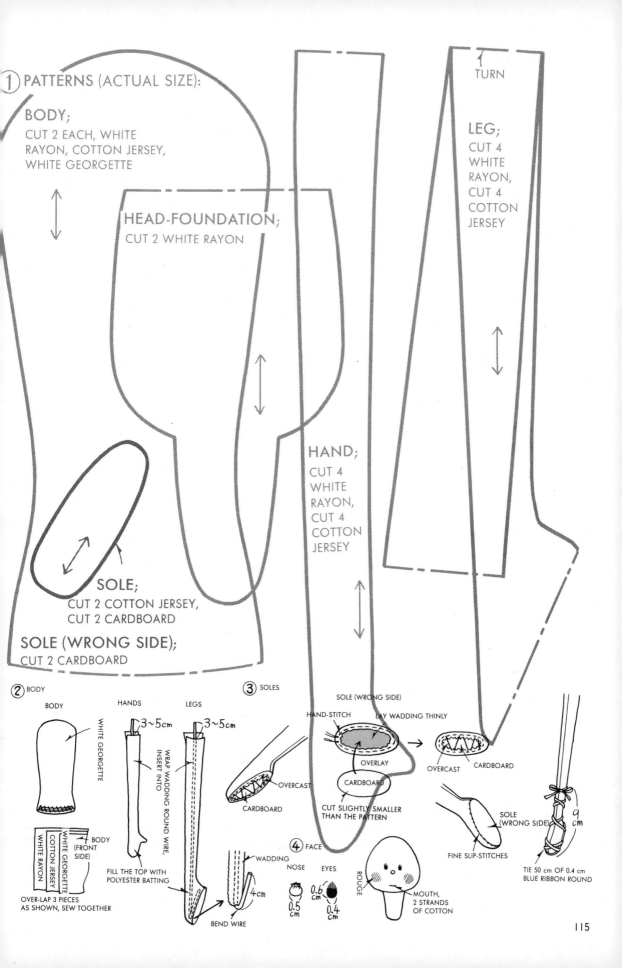

① PATTERNS (ACTUAL SIZE):

BODY;
CUT 2 EACH, WHITE RAYON, COTTON JERSEY, WHITE GEORGETTE

HEAD-FOUNDATION;
CUT 2 WHITE RAYON

LEG;
CUT 4 WHITE RAYON, CUT 4 COTTON JERSEY

TURN

HAND;
CUT 4 WHITE RAYON, CUT 4 COTTON JERSEY

SOLE;
CUT 2 COTTON JERSEY, CUT 2 CARDBOARD

SOLE (WRONG SIDE);
CUT 2 CARDBOARD

② BODY

BODY

WHITE GEORGETTE

HANDS   LEGS
3~5cm   3~5cm

WRAP WADDING ROUND WIRE, INSERT INTO

FILL THE TOP WITH POLYESTER BATTING

WHITE RAYON / COTTON JERSEY / WHITE GEORGETTE

BODY (FRONT SIDE)

OVER-LAP 3 PIECES AS SHOWN, SEW TOGETHER

③ SOLES

SOLE (WRONG SIDE)

HAND-STITCH   LAY WADDING THINLY

OVERCAST

CARDBOARD

OVERLAY

CARDBOARD

CUT SLIGHTLY SMALLER THAN THE PATTERN

OVERCAST   CARDBOARD

SOLE (WRONG SIDE)

FINE SLIP-STITCHES

9 cm

TIE 50 cm OF 0.4 cm BLUE RIBBON ROUND

WADDING

BEND WIRE   4cm

④ FACE

NOSE   EYES
0.5 cm   0.6 cm   0.4 cm

ROUGE

MOUTH, 2 STRANDS OF COTTON

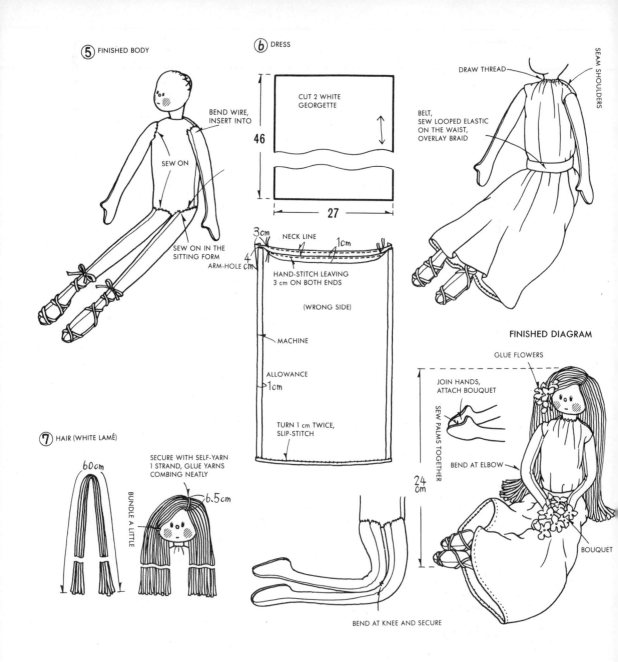

⑤ FINISHED BODY

BEND WIRE, INSERT INTO

SEW ON

SEW ON IN THE SITTING FORM

⑥ DRESS

CUT 2 WHITE GEORGETTE

46

27

3cm NECK LINE 1cm

ARM-HOLE cm 4

HAND-STITCH LEAVING 3 cm ON BOTH ENDS

(WRONG SIDE)

MACHINE

ALLOWANCE 1cm

TURN 1 cm TWICE, SLIP-STITCH

DRAW THREAD SEAM SHOULDERS

BELT, SEW LOOPED ELASTIC ON THE WAIST, OVERLAY BRAID

FINISHED DIAGRAM

GLUE FLOWERS

JOIN HANDS, ATTACH BOUQUET

SEW PALMS TOGETHER

BEND AT ELBOW

24 cm

BOUQUET

⑦ HAIR (WHITE LAMÉ)

60cm

BUNDLE A LITTLE

SECURE WITH SELF-YARN 1 STRAND, GLUE YARNS COMBING NEATLY

6.5cm

BEND AT KNEE AND SECURE

PACK

Shown on page 29.

Stuff packing neatly to give a smooth finish to the body. Feature the spirits of mischievous love-messenger in his posing.

YOU'LL NEED:
Head-Foundation, Body, Hands, Legs—60 cm by 32 cm White rayon. Face, Nose—12 cm by 15 cm Beige cotton jersey. Body, Hands, Legs—70 cm by 28 cm White cotton jersey. Eyes—Dacron georgette. Gold lame yarn. Mouth—Stranded embroidery thread. Hair —Loop yarn. And Others—Artificial leaves, Green taped wire. No. 18 wire. Packing. Cotton wadding. Polyester batting.
FINISHED SIZE: Refer to diagram.

MAKING INSTRUCTIONS:
Make body, hands, and legs with White jersey. As for the way to make hands and legs, refer to page 107. Attach soles after the Green wire is tied round legs. Hair is made of loop yarn softly crocheted with single crochet using No. 7/0 hook needle, and used its reverse side. Put polyester batting in the hair crocheted and lay over the head.
Apply leaves on the body, pose him bending hands and legs.

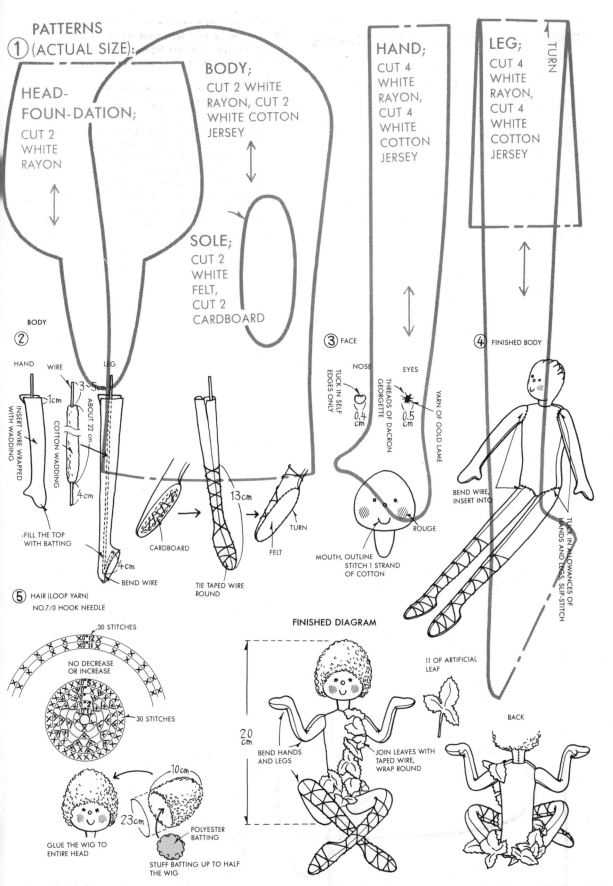

PATTERNS
① (ACTUAL SIZE):

HEAD-FOUN-DATION;
CUT 2 WHITE RAYON

BODY;
CUT 2 WHITE RAYON, CUT 2 WHITE COTTON JERSEY

SOLE;
CUT 2 WHITE FELT, CUT 2 CARDBOARD

HAND;
CUT 4 WHITE RAYON, CUT 4 WHITE COTTON JERSEY

LEG;
CUT 4 WHITE RAYON, CUT 4 WHITE COTTON JERSEY

TURN

② BODY

HAND
WIRE
LEG
BODY

3~5cm
1cm
ABOUT 22 cm
COTTON WADDING
4cm

INSERT WIRE WRAPPED WITH WADDING

FILL THE TOP WITH BATTING

4cm
BEND WIRE

CARDBOARD

13cm

TIE TAPED WIRE ROUND

TURN
FELT

③ FACE

TUCK IN SELF EDGES ONLY

NOSE
0.4 cm

THREADS OF DACRON GEORGETTE

EYES
0.5 cm

YARN OF GOLD LAME

ROUGE

MOUTH, OUTLINE STITCH 1 STRAND OF COTTON

④ FINISHED BODY

BEND WIRE, INSERT INTO

TUCK IN ALLOWANCES OF HANDS AND LEGS, SLIP-STITCH

⑤ HAIR (LOOP YARN)
NO.7/0 HOOK NEEDLE

30 STITCHES
X0"12X
X0"11X
NO DECREASE OR INCREASE
X0"5X
X0"4X
X0"3X
X0"2X
30 STITCHES

GLUE THE WIG TO ENTIRE HEAD

10cm
23cm
POLYESTER BATTING
STUFF BATTING UP TO HALF THE WIG

FINISHED DIAGRAM

20 cm

BEND HANDS AND LEGS

JOIN LEAVES WITH TAPED WIRE, WRAP ROUND

11 OF ARTIFICIAL LEAF

BACK

117

PIPPI WITH LONG STOCKINGS

Shown on page 30.

Though hands and legs look short in the picture, she really has a smart figure. Insert wire into the hair braided on sides and bend up to make her look rompish.

YOU'LL NEED:
Head-Foundation, Body, Hands, Legs—90 cm by 30 cm White rayon. Face, Nose, Hands—40 cm by 25 cm Beige cotton jersey. Legs—20 cm by 30 cm each, Black cotton jersey, Dark Brown cotton jersey. Eyes —Dacron georgette. Mouth—Stranded embroidery thread. Hair—Sport weight yarn. Dress, Bloomer— 55.5 cm by 24 cm dot print cotton. Stranded embroidery cotton. Scarf—30 cm by 12 cm cotton print. And Others—No. 18 wire. Packing. Cotton wadding. Polyester batting.

FINISHED SIZE: Refer to diagram.
MAKING INSTRUCTIONS:
Referring to page 50–64 for basic manner, make legs of Black and Dark Brown respecively.
Tuck garment at the center front, sew on decorated pocket, stitch side seams.
Sew on hair in same manner as for Hiji, insert wire into braided hair on sides and bend as shown.
Cut out scraf piece, wrap round neck.
Make shoes sewing on feet, finish with their tops bent upward. Bend legs if you like, securing at the knee back side in same manner as toe.

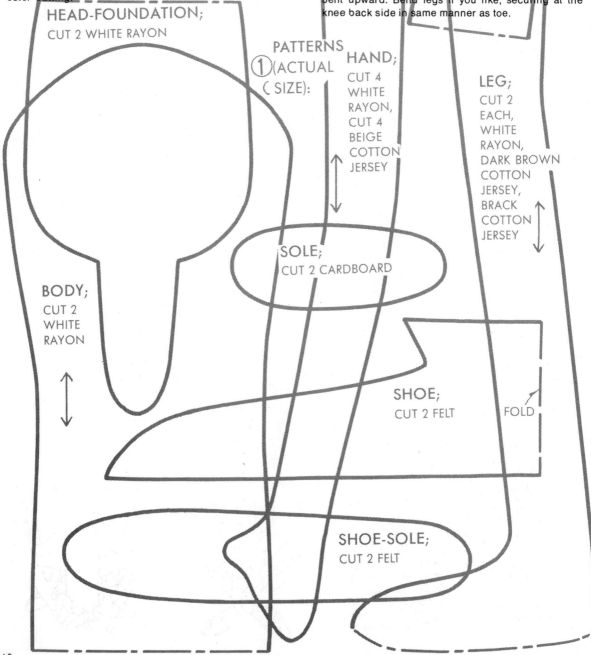

HEAD-FOUNDATION;
CUT 2 WHITE RAYON

PATTERNS
①(ACTUAL
(SIZE):

HAND;
CUT 4
WHITE
RAYON,
CUT 4
BEIGE
COTTON
JERSEY

LEG;
CUT 2
EACH,
WHITE
RAYON,
DARK BROWN
COTTON
JERSEY,
BRACK
COTTON
JERSEY

SOLE;
CUT 2 CARDBOARD

BODY;
CUT 2
WHITE
RAYON

SHOE;
CUT 2 FELT

FOLD

SHOE-SOLE;
CUT 2 FELT

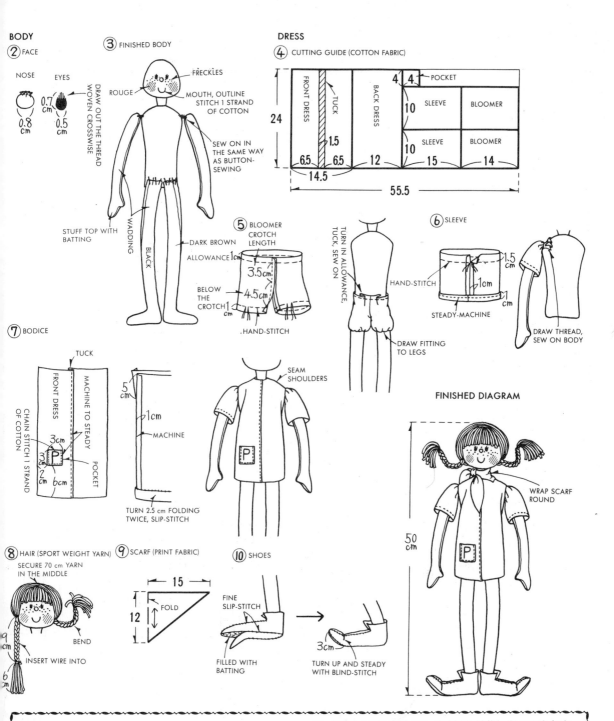

BODY

② FACE

NOSE

EYES

0.8 cm

0.7 cm

0.5 cm

DRAW OUT THE THREAD WOVEN CROSSWISE

③ FINISHED BODY

FRECKLES

ROUGE

MOUTH, OUTLINE STITCH 1 STRAND OF COTTON

SEW ON IN THE SAME WAY AS BUTTON-SEWING

STUFF TOP WITH BATTING

WADDING

BLACK

DARK BROWN

DRESS

④ CUTTING GUIDE (COTTON FABRIC)

FRONT DRESS

TUCK

BACK DRESS

4

4

POCKET

10

SLEEVE

BLOOMER

10

SLEEVE

BLOOMER

24

1.5

6.5

6.5

12

15

14

14.5

55.5

⑤ BLOOMER CROTCH LENGTH

ALLOWANCE 1cm

3.5cm

4.5cm

BELOW THE CROTCH 1cm

HAND-STITCH

TURN IN ALLOWANCE, TUCK, SEW ON

DRAW FITTING TO LEGS

⑥ SLEEVE

HAND-STITCH

STEADY-MACHINE

1.5 cm

1cm

DRAW THREAD, SEW ON BODY

⑦ BODICE

TUCK

FRONT DRESS

CHAIN STITCH 1 STRAND OF COTTON

MACHINE TO STEADY

POCKET

3cm

3 cm

2 cm

6cm

5 cm

1cm

MACHINE

TURN 2.5 cm FOLDING TWICE, SLIP-STITCH

SEAM SHOULDERS

P

FINISHED DIAGRAM

WRAP SCARF ROUND

P

50 cm

⑧ HAIR (SPORT WEIGHT YARN)

SECURE 70 cm YARN IN THE MIDDLE

BEND

INSERT WIRE INTO

⑨ SCARF (PRINT FABRIC)

15

12

FOLD

⑩ SHOES

FINE SLIP-STITCH

FILLED WITH BATTING

3cm

TURN UP AND STEADY WITH BLIND-STITCH

ROTTA

Shown on page 31.

To make a mischievous stubbon child, do rough hair-cut. Put on stockings as if right side slipped down loosely. The sweater beside him is only for an accessary at the place.

YOU 'LL NEED:

Head-Foundation, Body, Hands, Legs—90 cm by 14.5 cm White rayon. Face, Nose, Body, Hands, Legs—82 cm by 16 cm cotton jersey. Eyes—Dacron georgette. Mouth—Stranded embroidery thread. Hair—Mohair yarn. Shirt, Pants—13.5 cm by 36 cm cotton print. Stockings—Light weight yarn Pale Yellow, Olive Green. Sweater—Light weight yarn Grey. Pig—15 cm by 5 cm felt, dacron georgette. And Others—No. 18 wire. Packing. Cotton wadding. Polyester batting.

FINISHED SIZE: Refer to diagram.

MAKING INSTRUCTIONS:

Referring to page 50–64 for basic manner, make hands and legs in same manner as for Pack shown on page 117.

Sew on hair as shown on page 72, finish with ladder-

cut. The additional bundle is attached on sides and back.
Crochet sweater and stockings with hook needle size 1.

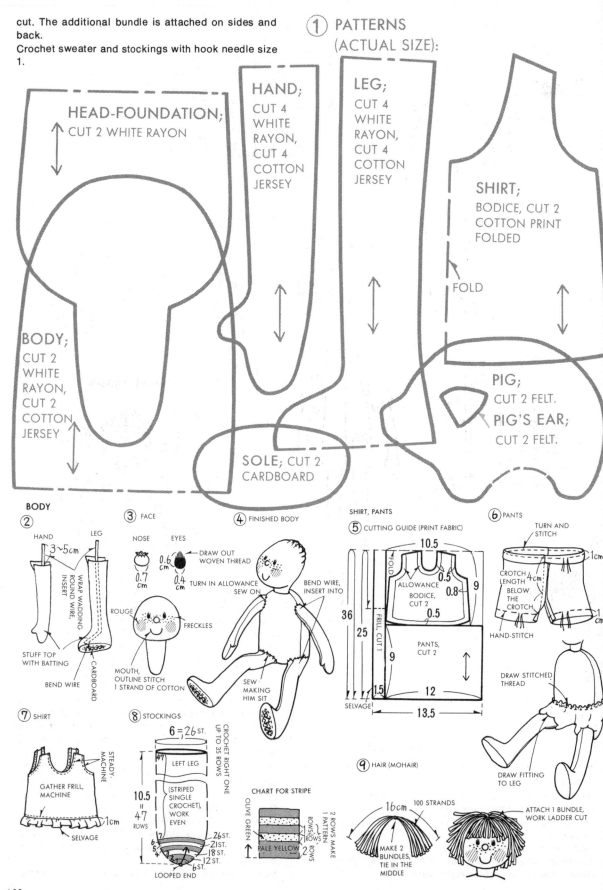

① PATTERNS (ACTUAL SIZE):

HEAD-FOUNDATION; CUT 2 WHITE RAYON

HAND; CUT 4 WHITE RAYON, CUT 4 COTTON JERSEY

LEG; CUT 4 WHITE RAYON, CUT 4 COTTON JERSEY

SHIRT; BODICE, CUT 2 COTTON PRINT FOLDED

FOLD

BODY; CUT 2 WHITE RAYON, CUT 2 COTTON JERSEY

PIG; CUT 2 FELT.

PIG'S EAR; CUT 2 FELT.

SOLE; CUT 2 CARDBOARD

BODY
②
HAND
LEG
3~5cm
WRAP WADDING ROUND WIRE, INSERT
STUFF TOP WITH BATTING
CARDBOARD
BEND WIRE

③ FACE
NOSE
EYES
0.7cm
0.6cm
0.4cm
DRAW OUT WOVEN THREAD
TURN IN ALLOWANCE SEW ON
ROUGE
FRECKLES
MOUTH, OUTLINE STITCH 1 STRAND OF COTTON

④ FINISHED BODY
BEND WIRE, INSERT INTO
SEW MAKING HIM SIT

SHIRT, PANTS
⑤ CUTTING GUIDE (PRINT FABRIC)
10.5
FOLD
ALLOWANCE
BODICE, CUT 2
0.5
0.8
0.5
9
36
25
FRILL CUT 1
PANTS, CUT 2
9
1.5
12
SELVAGE
13.5

⑥ PANTS
TURN AND STITCH
1cm
CROTCH LENGTH 4cm BELOW THE CROTCH
1cm
HAND-STITCH
DRAW STITCHED THREAD
DRAW FITTING TO LEG

⑦ SHIRT
STEADY-MACHINE
GATHER FRILL, MACHINE
1cm
SELVAGE

⑧ STOCKINGS
6 = 26 ST.
CROCHET RIGHT ONE UP TO 35 ROWS
47
LEFT LEG
10.5 = 47 ROWS
(STRIPED SINGLE CROCHET), WORK EVEN
26 ST.
21 ST.
18 ST.
12 ST.
6 ST.
LOOPED END

CHART FOR STRIPE
OLIVE GREEN
2 ROWS MAKE 1 PATTERN
PALE YELLOW

⑨ HAIR (MOHAIR)
16cm
100 STRANDS
MAKE 2 BUNDLES, TIE IN THE MIDDLE
ATTACH 1 BUNDLE, WORK LADDER CUT

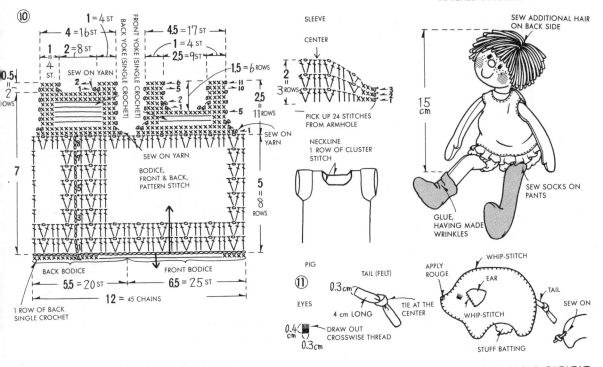

⑩

1 = 4 ST
4 = 16 ST
1 = 4 ST
2 = 8 ST

BACK YOKE (SINGLE CROCHET)
FRONT YOKE (SINGLE CROCHET)

4.5 = 17 ST
1 = 4 ST
2.5 = 9 ST

1.5 = 6 ROWS

0.5 / 2 / ROWS

1 4 ST.

SEW ON YARN

2.5 / 11 ROWS

5 / 8 ROWS

SEW ON YARN

7

SEW ON YARN

BODICE, FRONT & BACK, PATTERN STITCH

5 / 8 / ROWS

BACK BODICE

FRONT BODICE

5.5 = 20 ST

6.5 = 25 ST

12 = 45 CHAINS

1 ROW OF BACK SINGLE CROCHET

SLEEVE
CENTER

1 / 2 / 3 ROWS

PICK UP 24 STITCHES FROM ARMHOLE

NECKLINE
1 ROW OF CLUSTER STITCH

SEW ADDITIONAL HAIR ON BACK SIDE

15 cm

GLUE, HAVING MADE WRINKLES

SEW SOCKS ON PANTS

PIG
⑪

0.3cm
4 cm LONG
TIE AT THE CENTER

EYES
0.4 cm
0.3cm
DRAW OUT CROSSWISE THREAD

WHIP-STITCH
APPLY ROUGE
EAR
TAIL
SEW ON
WHIP-STITCH
STUFF BATTING

GYPSY-MAN

Shown on page 32.

Pay attention to the way to draw the thread of wrinkles on her face. Hair is made of the yarn unraveled from knit work. Feature her figure, making thick breast, waist, and hips.

YOU'LL NEED:
Head-Foundation, Body, Hands, Legs—82 cm by 24 cm White rayon. Face, Nose, Hands—35 cm by 17 cm Beige cotton jersey. Legs—28 cm by 12 cm Black cotton jersey. Eyes—Dacron georgette. Mouth—Stranded embroidery thread. Hair—White knitting cotton. Bloomer, Petticoat—90 cm by 16 cm White broad cloth. 98 cm of 2 cm White lace. Dress, Scarf—67 cm by 48 cm tricot print. 30 cm of 1.5 cm Black lace. Heavy weight yarn. Earrings—Silver and Black braid. Shoes—24 cm of 2.5 cm braid. Stole—No. 40 Black lace. Silver lame yarn. And Others—No. 12 silk necklace. No. 18 wire. Packing. Cotton wadding. Polyester batting.

FINISHED SIZE: Refer to diagram.
MAKING INSTRUCTIONS:
Referring to page 50–64 for basic manner, make hands and legs in same manner as for Prince on page 107.
Lay wadding over the face for more prominent cheeks and jaw, overlay skin fabric, stitch wrinkles with silk thread.
Lay wadding over the breast, waist, and hips to make them thick, sew on underwear and then dress.
Attach hair of the yarn unraveled from some knit work on the head as shown.
Crochet scarf with hook needle size 2.

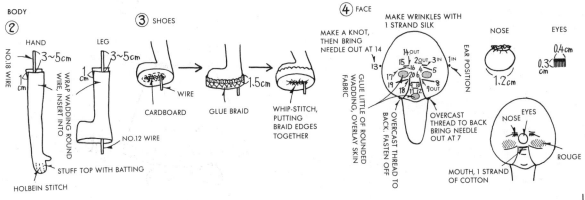

BODY ②

HAND
NO.18 WIRE
3~5cm
1 cm
WRAP WADDING ROUND WIRE, INSERT INTO

LEG
3~5cm
1 cm
NO.12 WIRE
STUFF TOP WITH BATTING
HOLBEIN STITCH

③ SHOES
CARDBOARD
WIRE
GLUE BRAID
1.5cm
WHIP-STITCH, PUTTING BRAID EDGES TOGETHER

④ FACE
MAKE WRINKLES WITH 1 STRAND SILK
MAKE A KNOT, THEN BRING NEEDLE OUT AT 14
GLUE LITTLE OF ROUNDED WADDING, OVERLAY SKIN FABRIC
EAR POSITION
OVERCAST THREAD TO BACK. FASTEN OFF
OVERCAST THREAD TO BACK BRING NEEDLE OUT AT 7
MOUTH, 1 STRAND OF COTTON

NOSE
1.2cm

EYES
0.4cm
0.3cm

NOSE
EYES
ROUGE

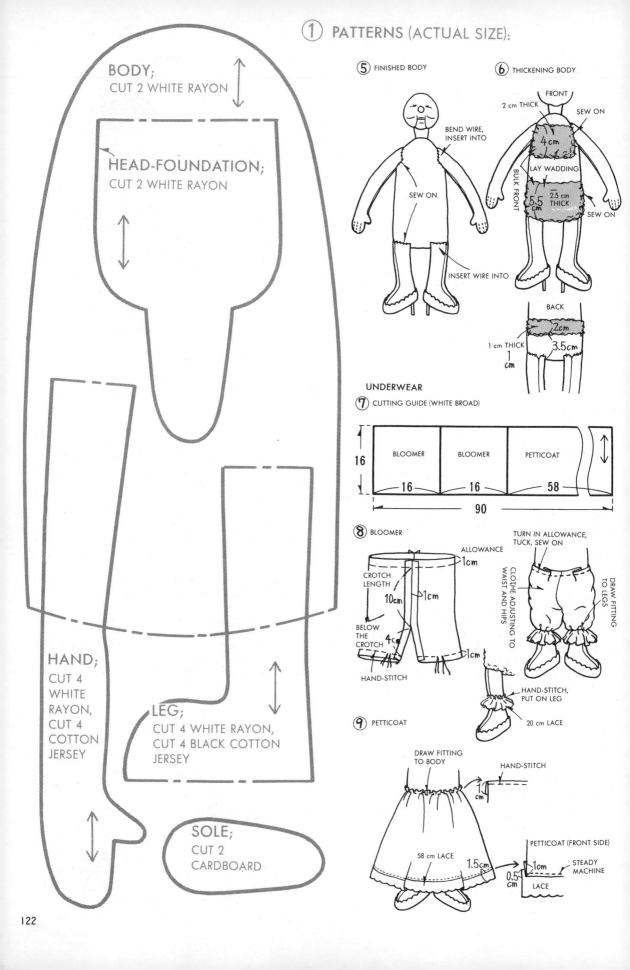

① PATTERNS (ACTUAL SIZE):

BODY;
CUT 2 WHITE RAYON

HEAD-FOUNDATION;
CUT 2 WHITE RAYON

HAND;
CUT 4
WHITE
RAYON,
CUT 4
COTTON
JERSEY

LEG;
CUT 4 WHITE RAYON,
CUT 4 BLACK COTTON
JERSEY

SOLE;
CUT 2
CARDBOARD

⑤ FINISHED BODY

BEND WIRE,
INSERT INTO

SEW ON

INSERT WIRE INTO

⑥ THICKENING BODY

FRONT
2 cm THICK
SEW ON
4cm
LAY WADDING
BULK FRONT
5.5 cm
2.5 cm THICK
SEW ON

BACK
2cm
1 cm THICK
3.5cm
1 cm

UNDERWEAR

⑦ CUTTING GUIDE (WHITE BROAD)

16	BLOOMER	BLOOMER	PETTICOAT	
	16	16	58	

90

⑧ BLOOMER

ALLOWANCE
1cm
CROTCH
LENGTH
10cm
1cm
BELOW
THE
CROTCH
4cm
1cm
HAND-STITCH

TURN IN ALLOWANCE,
TUCK, SEW ON
CLOTHE ADJUSTING TO
WAIST AND HIPS
DRAW FITTING
TO LEGS

HAND-STITCH,
PUT ON LEG
20 cm LACE

⑨ PETTICOAT

DRAW FITTING
TO BODY
HAND-STITCH
1 cm

58 cm LACE
1.5cm

PETTICOAT (FRONT SIDE)
1cm
STEADY
MACHINE
0.5 cm
LACE

DRESS

⑩ CUTTING GUIDE (TRICOT)

SLEEVE	SLEEVE
15	
13	13

48

18

SCARF

20.5   20.5

30

BODICE   BODICE

32   32

67

⑪ SLEEVE

2cm
0.8cm
HAND-STITCH
15 cm BLACK LACE
DRAW FITTING TO HAND

2 cm   0.5cm

TURN 1 cm FOLDING TWICE, SLIP-STITCH

DRAW THREAD

GATHER AND SEW ON

⑫ BODICE

3.5cm
STITCH NECKLINE FRONT AND BACK

5 cm

BODICE (WRONG SIDE)

MACHINE SIDE SEAM   1cm

DRAW FITTING TO NECK

5cm

SEAM

DRAW WAIST WITH THE LACE TIED ROUND

TURN 3 cm FOLDING TWICE, SLIP-STITCH

⑬ EARRINGS

SEW ON

TIE

1.5cm

10 cm OF BRAID

⑭ HAIR

YARN UNRAVELED FROM KNIT WORK

APPLY GLUE ENTIRE HEAD, ATTACH YARN

⑮ STOLE

27cm

10   CENTER   9   5   2 1   SEW ON THREAD

12 cm

▲ = FRINGE HERE

FINISHED DIAGRAM

SCARF, TURN IN 1 cm, GLUE TO POSITION

TIE ON BACK

NECK-LACE

SCARF

HAIR

33 cm

BEND AT ELBOW

STRING, BRAID 2 STRANDS OF HEAVY WEIGHT YARN TOGETHER

53cm
2cm   2cm

KNOTS OF FRINGE

5.5cm

EDGE YARN

12 cm LACE YARN 3 STRANDS

KNOT 2 OF 3 STRANDS TOGETHER

X·o·丁 = THE YARN OF LACE AND SILVER LAMÉ STRANDED

X·o·丅 = LACE YARN 1 STRAND

A WITCH UNDER THE NEW MOON

Shown on page 33.

Her broomstick is made of tree branch. Try to hang the doll in the air with the string tied on her head. You may enjoy its flying figure.

YOU'LL NEED:
Head-Foundation, Body, Hands, Legs—77 cm by 25 cm White rayon. Face, Nose, Hands—32 cm by 22 cm Beige cotton jersey. Legs—28 cm by 25 cm Black cotton jersey. Eyes—Dacron georgette. Mouth—Stranded embroidery thread. Hair—Frizzle yarn. Glasses—Black wire. Dress—46 cm by cm Black cotton jersey. Cap—19 cm by 16 cm Black felt. Broom—45 cm of tree branch. 17 cm square linen. And Others—Packing. Cotton wadding. Polyester batting. Silk thread. No. 18 wire.

FINISHED SIZE: Refer to diagram.
MAKING INSTRUCTIONS:
Referring to page 50–64 for basic manner, make hands and legs in same manner as for Stray Angels shown on page 110. Make wrinkles on her face with silk thread.
Having sleeves sewn on hands, set arms in position. Sew on hair referring to page 72.

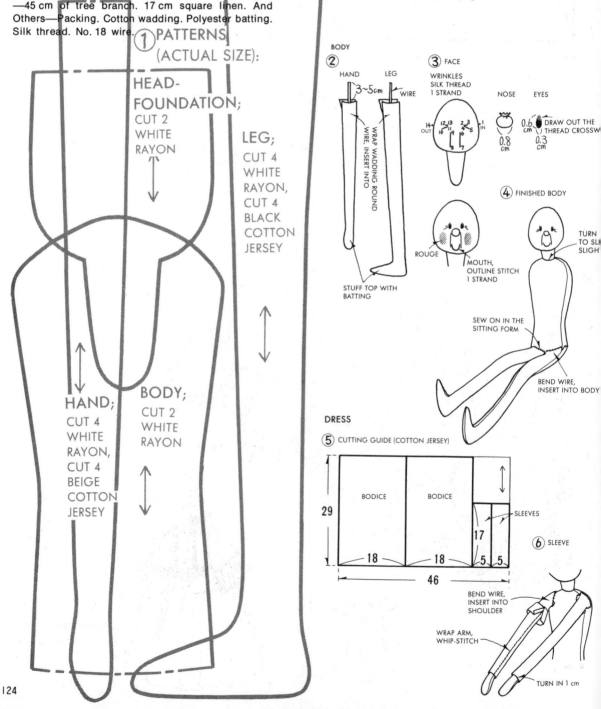

① PATTERNS (ACTUAL SIZE):

HEAD-FOUNDATION; CUT 2 WHITE RAYON

LEG; CUT 4 WHITE RAYON, CUT 4 BLACK COTTON JERSEY

HAND; CUT 4 WHITE RAYON, CUT 4 BEIGE COTTON JERSEY

BODY; CUT 2 WHITE RAYON

BODY

② HAND LEG WIRE 3~5cm

WRAP WADDING ROUND WIRE, INSERT INTO

STUFF TOP WITH BATTING

③ FACE WRINKLES SILK THREAD 1 STRAND

NOSE 0.8 cm

EYES 0.6 cm DRAW OUT THE THREAD CROSSW 0.3 cm

ROUGE

MOUTH, OUTLINE STITCH 1 STRAND

④ FINISHED BODY

TURN TO SLI SLIGH

SEW ON IN THE SITTING FORM

BEND WIRE, INSERT INTO BODY

DRESS

⑤ CUTTING GUIDE (COTTON JERSEY)

BODICE	BODICE		SLEEVES

29
18 18 5 5
17
46

⑥ SLEEVE

BEND WIRE, INSERT INTO SHOULDER

WRAP ARM, WHIP-STITCH

TURN IN 1 cm

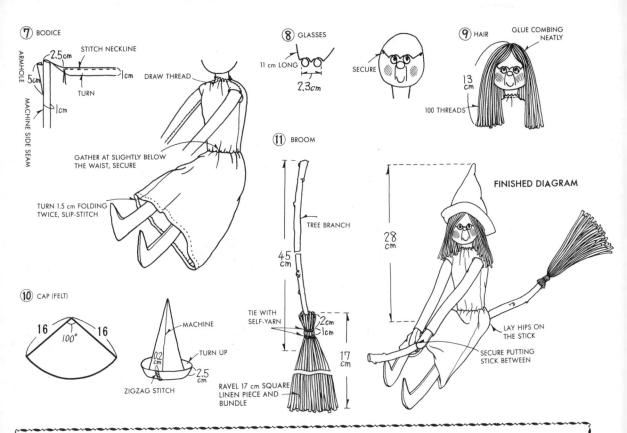

⑦ BODICE

STITCH NECKLINE

2.5cm

ARMHOLE

5cm

TURN

1cm

MACHINE SIDE SEAM

1cm

DRAW THREAD

GATHER AT SLIGHTLY BELOW THE WAIST, SECURE

TURN 1.5 cm FOLDING TWICE, SLIP-STITCH

⑧ GLASSES

11 cm LONG

2.3cm

SECURE

⑨ HAIR

GLUE COMBING NEATLY

13 cm

100 THREADS

⑪ BROOM

TREE BRANCH

45 cm

TIE WITH SELF-YARN

2cm
1cm

17 cm

RAVEL 17 cm SQUARE LINEN PIECE AND BUNDLE

FINISHED DIAGRAM

28 cm

LAY HIPS ON THE STICK

SECURE PUTTING STICK BETWEEN

⑩ CAP (FELT)

16   16

100°

MACHINE

TURN UP

0.2

2.5 cm

ZIGZAG STITCH

AUNT KETTY

Shown on page 34.

Hairs are unraveled old yarn. Let her stand, making holes on the board higher than 2.5 cm with gimlet. Make wrinkles drawing thread slightly.

YOU'LL NEED:

Head-Foundation, Body, Hands—47 cm by 27 cm White rayon. Face, Nose, Hands—50 cm by 27 cm cotton jersey. Legs—18 cm by 28 cm striped cotton. Eyes—Dacron georgette. Mouth—Stranded embroidery thread. Hair—Mohair yarn. Glasses—Grey wire. Bloomer, Petticoat, Apron, Blouse's collar, Front Placket—62 cm by 23 cm White broad. 51 cm of 2.5 cm White lace. 13 cm of 1.5 cm White lace. Blouse —37 cm by 18.5 cm cotton seersucker. 25 cm of 3 cm lace. Skirt—32 cm by 23.5 cm denim. Shoes—26 cm by 3 cm velveteen. 5 cm by 4 cm felt. And Others—

Wire No. 12, No. 18. Packing. Cotton wadding. Polyester batting. Silk thread.

FINISHED SIZE: Refer to diagram.

MAKING INSTRUCTIONS:

Make referring to page 50–64 for basic manner. The face is skined after wadding piece is laid on cheeks and jaw, then stitch wrinkles with silk thread. Make hands and legs with the wire inserted. Shoes are made as shown on page 90. As for the hair, use the yarn unraveled from knit goods, putting on the head attached with glue.

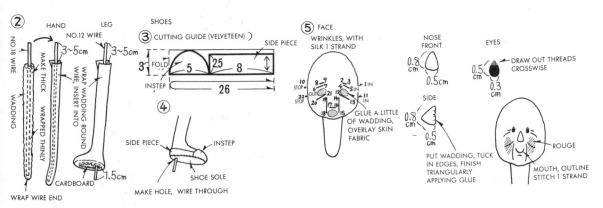

② HAND LEG

NO.18 WIRE

MAKE THICK WRAPPED THINLY

NO.12 WIRE

3~5cm   3~5cm

WRAP WADDING ROUND WIRE, INSERT INTO

WADDING

CARDBOARD

1.5cm

WRAP WIRE END

③ CUTTING GUIDE (VELVETEEN)

SHOES

SIDE PIECE

3 FOLD

5   25   8

INSTEP

26

④

SIDE PIECE   INSTEP

SHOE SOLE

MAKE HOLE, WIRE THROUGH

⑤ FACE

WRINKLES, WITH SILK 1 STRAND

GLUE A LITTLE OF WADDING, OVERLAY SKIN FABRIC

NOSE

FRONT

0.8 cm

0.5cm

SIDE

0.8 cm

0.5

PUT WADDING, TUCK IN EDGES, FINISH TRIANGULARLY APPLYING GLUE

EYES

DRAW OUT THREADS CROSSWISE

0.5 cm

0.3 cm

ROUGE

MOUTH, OUTLINE STITCH 1 STRAND

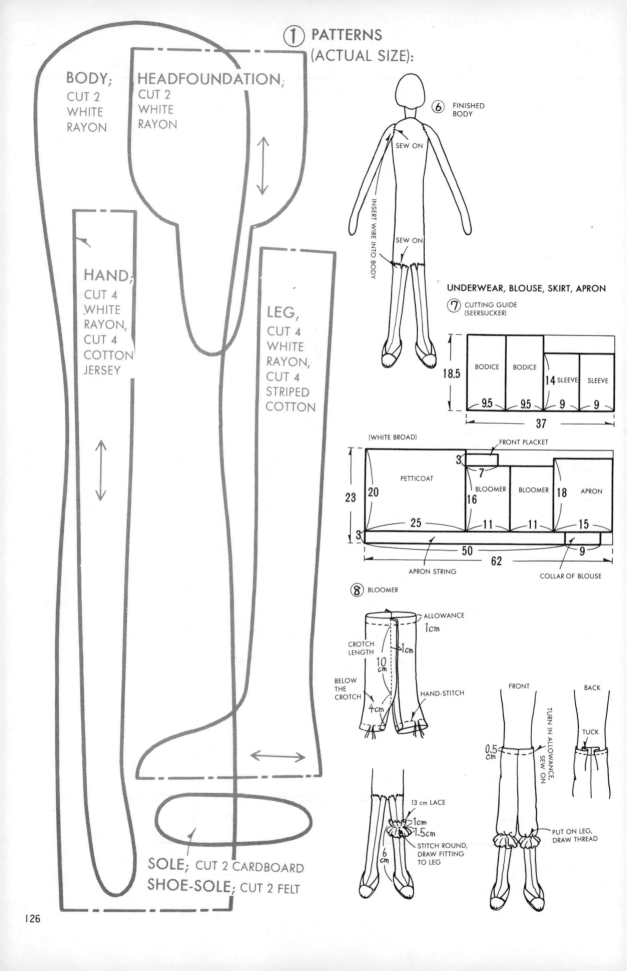

① PATTERNS
(ACTUAL SIZE):

BODY; CUT 2 WHITE RAYON

HEADFOUNDATION; CUT 2 WHITE RAYON

HAND; CUT 4 WHITE RAYON, CUT 4 COTTON JERSEY

LEG, CUT 4 WHITE RAYON, CUT 4 STRIPED COTTON

SOLE; CUT 2 CARDBOARD
SHOE-SOLE; CUT 2 FELT

⑥ FINISHED BODY

INSERT WIRE INTO BODY

SEW ON

SEW ON

UNDERWEAR, BLOUSE, SKIRT, APRON

⑦ CUTTING GUIDE (SEERSUCKER)

(WHITE BROAD)

BODICE 9.5	BODICE 9.5	14 SLEEVE 9	SLEEVE 9

18.5 — 37

| PETTICOAT 20 | 3 7 BLOOMER 16 | BLOOMER | 18 APRON |

23 — 3 — 25 — 11 — 11 — 15

50 — 62 — 9

FRONT PLACKET

APRON STRING

COLLAR OF BLOUSE

⑧ BLOOMER

ALLOWANCE 1cm

CROTCH LENGTH 10 cm 1cm

BELOW THE CROTCH 4cm

HAND-STITCH

FRONT

TURN IN ALLOWANCE, SEW ON

0.5 cm

BACK

TUCK

13 cm LACE
1cm
1.5cm

STITCH ROUND, DRAW FITTING TO LEG

6 cm

PUT ON LEG, DRAW THREAD

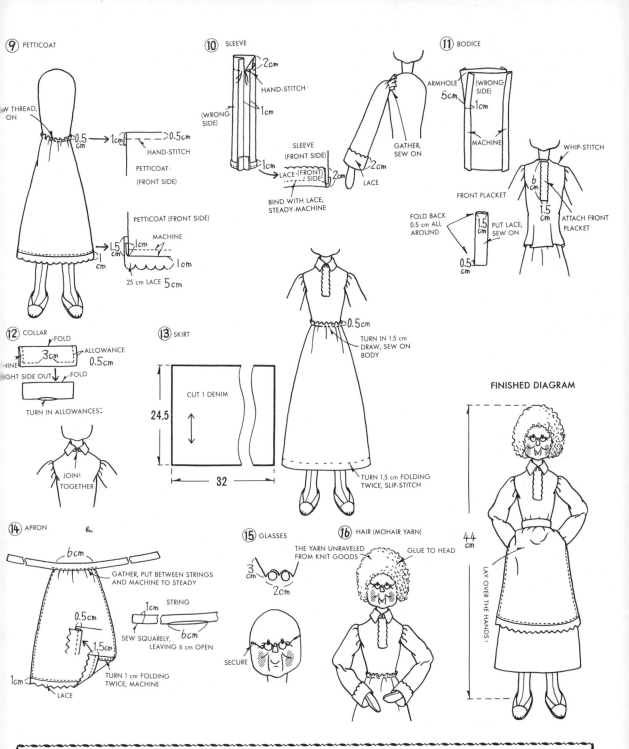

⑨ PETTICOAT

W THREAD, ON

0.5 cm → 1cm → 0.5 cm

HAND-STITCH

PETTICOAT (FRONT SIDE)

PETTICOAT (FRONT SIDE)

1.5 cm   MACHINE   1cm

25 cm LACE   5cm

⑩ SLEEVE

2cm

HAND-STITCH

(WRONG SIDE)

1cm

1cm

SLEEVE (FRONT SIDE)

LACE (FRONT SIDE)

BIND WITH LACE, STEADY-MACHINE

GATHER, SEW ON

SLEEVE (FRONT SIDE)

2cm

2cm

LACE

⑪ BODICE

ARMHOLE   5cm

(WRONG SIDE)   1cm

MACHINE

FRONT PLACKET

FOLD BACK 0.5 cm ALL AROUND

1.5 cm

0.5 cm

WHIP-STITCH

6 cm

1.5 cm

ATTACH FRONT PLACKET

PUT LACE, SEW ON

⑫ COLLAR

FOLD

3cm   ALLOWANCE

HINE   0.5cm

GHT SIDE OUT   FOLD

TURN IN ALLOWANCES

JOIN TOGETHER

⑬ SKIRT

CUT 1 DENIM

24.5

32

0.5 cm

TURN IN 1.5 cm DRAW, SEW ON BODY

TURN 1.5 cm FOLDING TWICE, SLIP-STITCH

FINISHED DIAGRAM

44 cm

LAY OVER THE HANDS !

⑭ APRON

6cm

GATHER, PUT BETWEEN STRINGS AND MACHINE TO STEADY

0.5 cm

1cm   STRING

SEW SQUARELY, LEAVING 6 cm OPEN

6cm

1.5 cm

1cm   TURN 1 cm FOLDING TWICE, MACHINE

LACE

⑮ GLASSES

3 cm

2cm

SECURE

⑯ HAIR (MOHAIR YARN)

THE YARN UNRAVELED FROM KNIT GOODS   GLUE TO HEAD

MISS. BRENDA

Shown on page 35.

The skirt is decorated with White laces attached with shirring. The making manner is basically same as for Hiji. Put Black stockings on her legs with Black georgette using as a skin fabric.

YOU'LL NEED:
Head-Foundation, Body, Hands, Legs—86 cm by 58 cm White rayon. Face, Nose, Hands—55 cm by 30 cm Beige georgette. Legs—42 cm by 35 cm Black georgette. Eyes—Dacron georgette. Mouth—Stranded embroidery thread. Hair—Loop yarn. Bloomer,

Petticoat—84 cm by 29 cm White broad. 50 cm of 2 cm lace. Dress—55 cm by 33.5 cm gingham check. 85 cm by 29 cm gingham check smaller plaid. 630 cm of 2 cm lace ribbon. Shoes—70 cm of 1 cm Black braid. 9 cm by 6.5 cm Black felt. And Others—Packing. Cotton wadding. Polyester batting.

FINISHED SIZE: Refer to diagram.
MAKING INSTRUCTIONS:
Make referring to page 50–64 for basic manner.
Stuff legs firmly with polyester batting.
Sew lace ribbon on the skirt (b), shirr it into 55 cm

wide.
Stitch shirred lace ribbon to sleeve end, sew under-arm seam together.
Sew hairs on the head all over in same manner as shown on page 67.

① PATTERNS (ACTUAL SIZE):

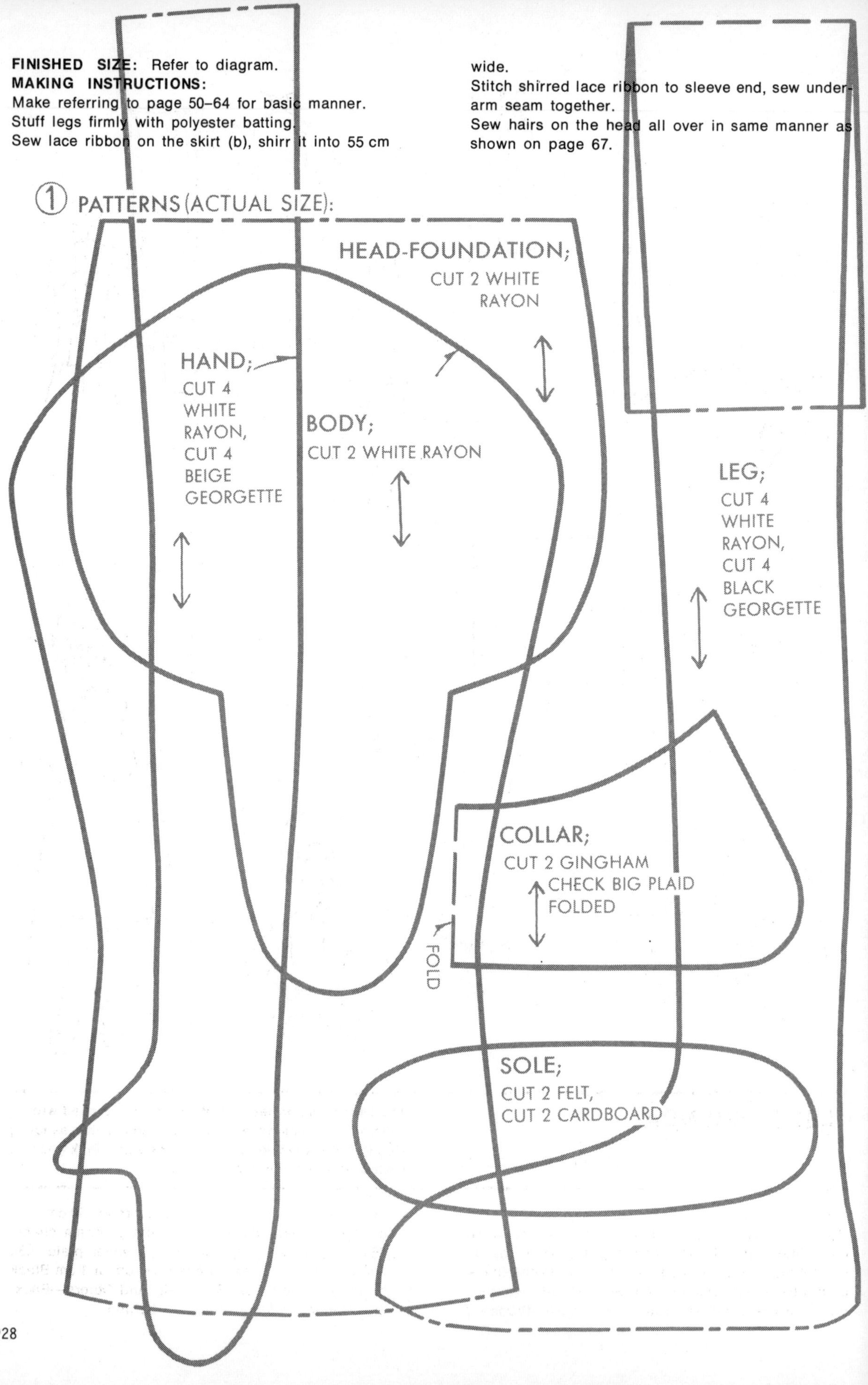

HEAD-FOUNDATION;
CUT 2 WHITE RAYON

HAND;
CUT 4 WHITE RAYON,
CUT 4 BEIGE GEORGETTE

BODY;
CUT 2 WHITE RAYON

LEG;
CUT 4 WHITE RAYON,
CUT 4 BLACK GEORGETTE

COLLAR;
CUT 2 GINGHAM CHECK BIG PLAID FOLDED

FOLD

SOLE;
CUT 2 FELT,
CUT 2 CARDBOARD

BODY

② SHOES

STUFF BATTING

CARDBOARD

BRAID

FELT

③ FACE

NOSE

0.8 cm

EYES

0.8 cm

0.5 cm

DRAW OUT WOVEN THREADS

④ FINISHED BODY

FRECKLES

ROUGE

MOUTH, 2 STRANDS COTTON

SEW ON SAME AS BUTTON-SEWING

POLYESTER BATTING

UNDERWEAR

⑤ CUTTING GUIDE (WHITE BROAD)

PETTICOAT

BLOOMER

BLOOMER

29

24

50

17

17

84

⑥ BLOOMER

ALLOWANCE 1cm

CROTCH LENGTH 4.5 cm

(WRONG SIDE)

BELOW THE CROTCH 17.5 cm

HAND-STITCH

1cm

TURN IN ALLOWANCE TUCK, SECURE

PUT ON LEGS, DRAW THREAD

⑦ PETTICOAT

HAND-STITCH

0.5 cm

1cm

(RIGHT SIDE)

(RIGHT SIDE)

MACHINE

1cm

0.5 cm

LACE

1.5 cm

DRESS

⑧ CUTTING GUIDE (LARGE PLAID GINGHAM)

CUT 2 SLEEVES

COLLAR

CUT 2 BODICE

24.5

18.5

33.5

12

13

9

ⓐ SKIRT

FOLD

55

SHIRR ALONG LACES

⑨ SKIRT

ⓑ SKIRT

SMALLER PLAID GINGHAM

SEW ON LACE RIBBON

1.5 cm

2 cm

29 cm

2cm

2cm

1.5 cm

85 cm

SHIRR INTO 55 cm

MACHINE AND PRESS OPEN

ⓐ SKIRT (RIGHT SIDE)

1.5 cm

1.5 cm

SKIRT (RIGHT SIDE)

ⓑ SKIRT (RIGHT SIDE)

1.5 cm

1cm

MACHINE

ⓐ SKIRT

1cm

HAND-STITCH, PUT ON BODY, DRAW THREAD, SECURE

ⓐ SKIRT

LACE

ⓑ SKIRT

⑩ SLEEVE

2cm

1 cm

HAND-STITCH

(RIGHT SIDE)

2cm

SEAM AFTER THE SLEEVE END IS LACED

SHIRR 17 cm OF LACE RIBBON INTO 12 cm

2cm

ALLOWANCE STEADY-MACHINE

GATHER AND SEW ON

⑪ BODICE

SEAM SHOULDERS AND SIDES

⑫ COLLAR

OPENING FOR TURNING

0.6cm

MACHINE

1cm

JOIN COLLARS

⑬ HAIR (LOOP YARN)

WIND 5 TIMES

SEW ON ENTIRE HEAD

FINISHED DIAGRAM

65 cm

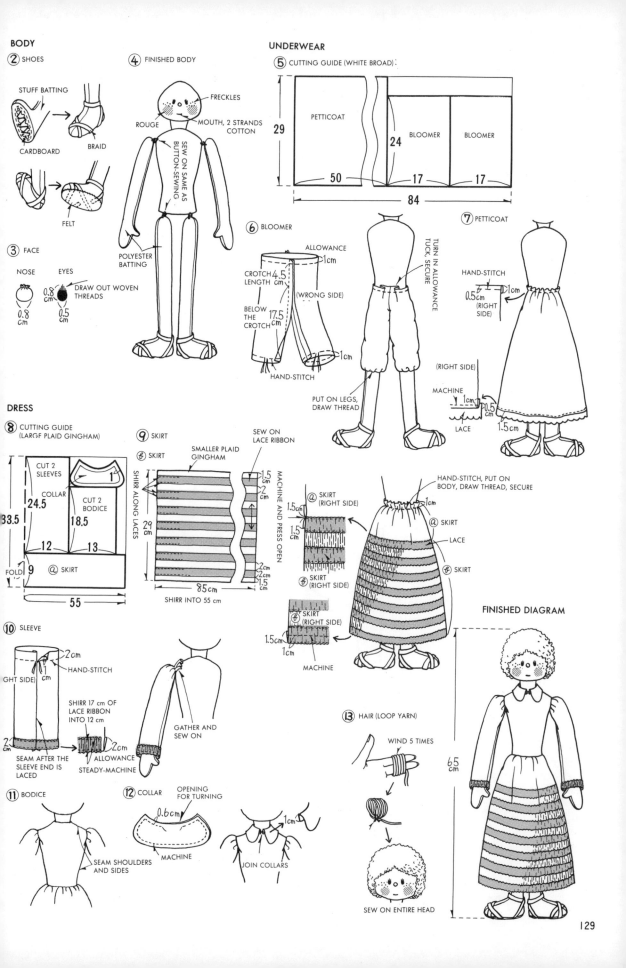

129

AT HOME ON A RAINY DAY

Shown on page 37.

The make of her legs is distinctive. Use fine thread of skin color. Set up her pose at the stage of foundation making. Set in head with her face turned sideways slightly.

YOU'LL NEED:
Head-Foundation, Body, Hands, Legs—80 cm by 38 cm White rayon. Face, Nose, Hands, Legs—70 cm by 30 cm cotton jersey. Eyes—Dacron georgette. Mouth—Stranded embroidery thread. Hair—Sport weight yarn. Kimono—77 cm by 30 cm cotton print. Belt—72 cm by 10 cm broad cloth. And Others—No. 18 wire. Packing. Cotton wadding. Polyester batting.
FINISHED SIZE: Refer to diagram.

MAKING INSTRUCTIONS:
Referring to page 50–64 for basic manner, make hands and legs in same manner as for Pack shown on page 117.
Make toes with their big toes sewn on top as shown. Sew kimono referring to page 105–106, tie belt round, make her pose bending hands and legs.
Sew on hair as shown on page 72.

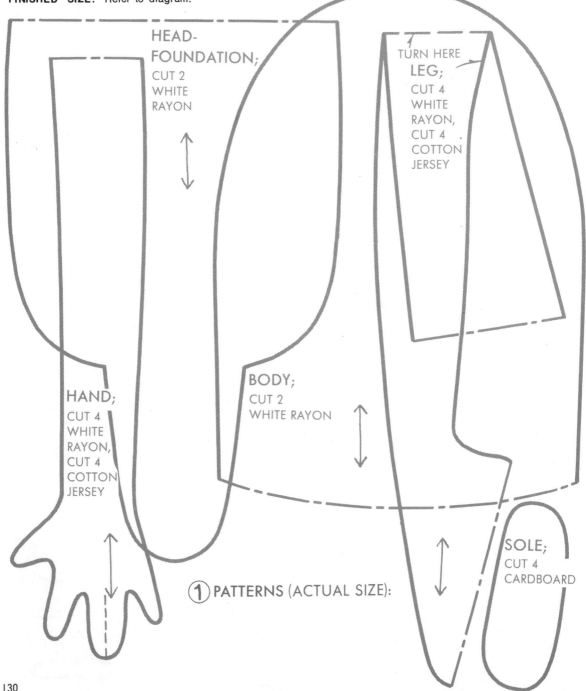

HEAD-FOUNDATION;
CUT 2
WHITE
RAYON

TURN HERE
LEG;
CUT 4
WHITE
RAYON,
CUT 4
COTTON
JERSEY

HAND;
CUT 4
WHITE
RAYON,
CUT 4
COTTON
JERSEY

BODY;
CUT 2
WHITE RAYON

SOLE;
CUT 4
CARDBOARD

① PATTERNS (ACTUAL SIZE):

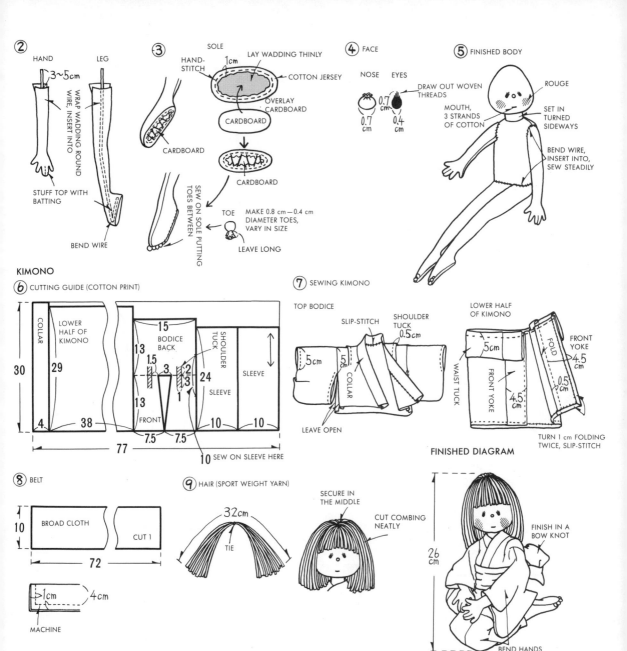

② HAND / LEG

3~5cm

WRAP WADDING ROUND WIRE, INSERT INTO

STUFF TOP WITH BATTING

BEND WIRE

③ SOLE / HAND-STITCH / LAY WADDING THINLY / 1cm / COTTON JERSEY / OVERLAY CARDBOARD / CARDBOARD

CARDBOARD

CARDBOARD

SEW ON SOLE PUTTING TOES BETWEEN

TOE / MAKE 0.8 cm — 0.4 cm DIAMETER TOES, VARY IN SIZE

LEAVE LONG

④ FACE / NOSE / EYES

0.7 cm / 0.7 cm / 0.4 cm

DRAW OUT WOVEN THREADS

MOUTH, 3 STRANDS OF COTTON

⑤ FINISHED BODY / ROUGE / SET IN TURNED SIDEWAYS / BEND WIRE, INSERT INTO, SEW STEADILY

KIMONO

⑥ CUTTING GUIDE (COTTON PRINT)

COLLAR / LOWER HALF OF KIMONO / 15 / BODICE BACK / SHOULDER TUCK / SLEEVE

30 / 29 / 13 / 1.5 / 3 / 2 / 3 / 24 / SLEEVE / 13 / 1 / 4 / 38 / FRONT / 10 / 10 / 7.5 / 7.5 / 77 / 10 SEW ON SLEEVE HERE

⑦ SEWING KIMONO

TOP BODICE / SLIP-STITCH / SHOULDER TUCK 0.5cm / 5cm / 5cm / COLLAR / LEAVE OPEN

LOWER HALF OF KIMONO / 5cm / FRONT YOKE / 4.5 cm / FOLD / WAIST TUCK / FRONT YOKE / 4.5 cm / 0.5 cm / TURN 1 cm FOLDING TWICE, SLIP-STITCH

FINISHED DIAGRAM

⑧ BELT

10 / BROAD CLOTH / CUT 1 / 72

1cm / 4cm / MACHINE

⑨ HAIR (SPORT WEIGHT YARN)

32cm / TIE

SECURE IN THE MIDDLE / CUT COMBING NEATLY

26 cm / FINISH IN A BOW KNOT / BEND HANDS AND LEGS

RAPUNZUEL

Shown on page 38.

This is a very simple cardboard-frame-doll. Attach hairs of embroidery floss or the yarn of bright Yellow combing neatly with tooth brush or the sort of thing.

YOU'LL NEED:
Head-Foundation, Body, Hands—60 cm by 13 cm White rayon. Face, Nose, Hands—40 cm by 14 cm cotton jersey. Frame—26 cm by 18 cm cardboard. 35 cm by 20 cm White rayon. Eyes—Dacron georgette. Mouth—Stranded embroidery thread. Hair—Stranded embroidery cotton 3 shades of Yellow. Floral braid. Petticoat—40 cm by 14 cm White broadcloth. 40 cm of 2 cm lace. Dress—44 cm by 44 cm cotton cm by 11 cm dacron seersucker. 95 cm of 2 cm lace. And Others—No. 18 wire. Packing. Cotton wadding. Polyester batting.
FINISHED SIZE: Refer to diagram.

MAKING INSTRUCTIONS:
Make referring to page 50–64 for basic manner.
As for the way to form and to set in hands, refer to page 110.
Make frame and sew on body. Sew frame cover, lay on the frame as shown.
Lay wadding thinly over the body, sew on bodice and work cross stitch at center front.
Sew apron on the waist, put lace ribbon over, glue and tie on back.
Make hair putting 3 shades of stranded embroidery cotton together, fasten in the middle, secure to head.
Make hair ornament, apply on the hair.

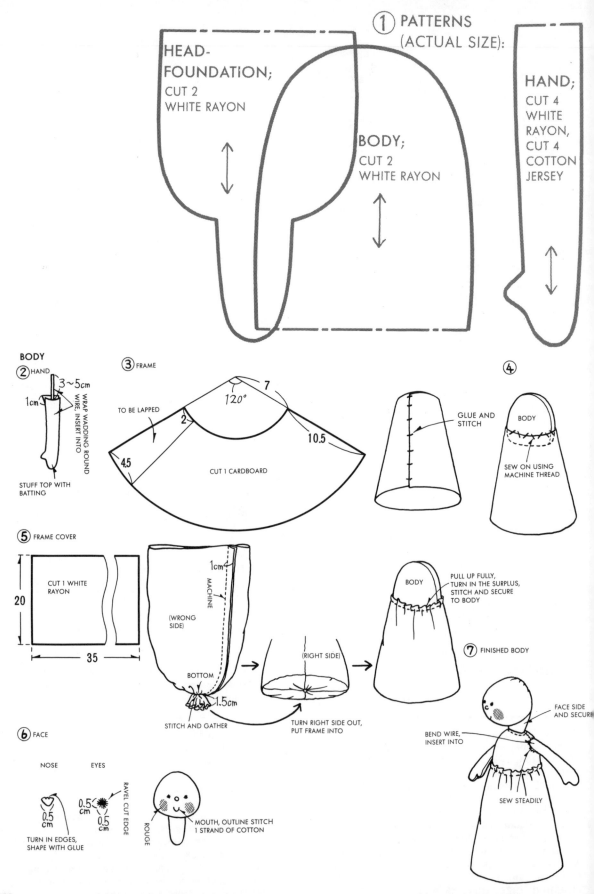

① PATTERNS (ACTUAL SIZE):

HEAD-FOUNDATION;
CUT 2
WHITE RAYON

BODY;
CUT 2
WHITE RAYON

HAND;
CUT 4
WHITE
RAYON,
CUT 4
COTTON
JERSEY

BODY

② HAND

3~5cm
1cm

WRAP WADDING ROUND WIRE, INSERT INTO

STUFF TOP WITH BATTING

③ FRAME

7
120°
TO BE LAPPED
2
4.5
10.5
CUT 1 CARDBOARD

④

GLUE AND STITCH

BODY

SEW ON USING MACHINE THREAD

⑤ FRAME COVER

CUT 1 WHITE RAYON

20
35

1cm
MACHINE
(WRONG SIDE)
BOTTOM
1.5cm
STITCH AND GATHER

(RIGHT SIDE)

TURN RIGHT SIDE OUT, PUT FRAME INTO

BODY

PULL UP FULLY, TURN IN THE SURPLUS, STITCH AND SECURE TO BODY

⑦ FINISHED BODY

⑥ FACE

NOSE

0.5 cm

TURN IN EDGES, SHAPE WITH GLUE

EYES

0.5 cm
0.5 cm

RAVEL CUT EDGE

ROUGE

MOUTH, OUTLINE STITCH 1 STRAND OF COTTON

FACE SIDE AND SECURE

BEND WIRE, INSERT INTO

SEW STEADILY

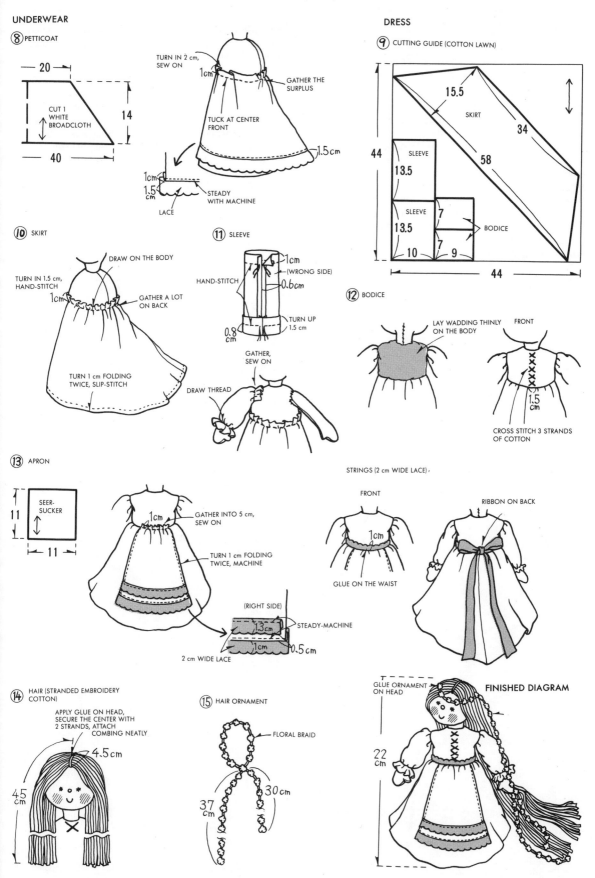

UNDERWEAR

⑧ PETTICOAT

20

CUT 1 WHITE BROADCLOTH

14

40

TURN IN 2 cm, SEW ON

1cm

GATHER THE SURPLUS

TUCK AT CENTER FRONT

1.5 cm

1cm
1.5 cm

LACE

STEADY WITH MACHINE

⑩ SKIRT

DRAW ON THE BODY

TURN IN 1.5 cm, HAND-STITCH

1cm

GATHER A LOT ON BACK

TURN 1 cm FOLDING TWICE, SLIP-STITCH

⑪ SLEEVE

1cm
(WRONG SIDE)

HAND-STITCH

0.6cm

TURN UP 1.5 cm

0.8 cm

GATHER, SEW ON

DRAW THREAD

DRESS

⑨ CUTTING GUIDE (COTTON LAWN)

15.5

SKIRT

34

44

SLEEVE
13.5

58

SLEEVE
13.5

7

BODICE

10

7

9

44

⑫ BODICE

LAY WADDING THINLY ON THE BODY

FRONT

1.5 cm

CROSS STITCH 3 STRANDS OF COTTON

STRINGS (2 cm WIDE LACE)

FRONT

1cm

GLUE ON THE WAIST

RIBBON ON BACK

⑬ APRON

11

SEER-SUCKER

11

1cm

GATHER INTO 5 cm, SEW ON

TURN 1 cm FOLDING TWICE, MACHINE

(RIGHT SIDE)

3 cm

STEADY-MACHINE

1cm

0.5 cm

2 cm WIDE LACE

⑭ HAIR (STRANDED EMBROIDERY COTTON)

APPLY GLUE ON HEAD, SECURE THE CENTER WITH 2 STRANDS, ATTACH COMBING NEATLY

4.5 cm

45 cm

⑮ HAIR ORNAMENT

FLORAL BRAID

30 cm

37 cm

GLUE ORNAMENT ON HEAD

FINISHED DIAGRAM

22 cm

133

PRINCESS ERRISSA

Shown on page 39.

Ready thick cardboard for the frame if available. Make the doll most princesslike, using gorgeous fabrics with fancy ribbons.

YOU'LL NEED:

Head-Foundation, Body, Hands—45 cm by 23 cm White rayon. Face, Nose, Hands—30 cm by 22 cm georgette. Frame—33 cm by 33 cm cardboard. 40 cm by 35 cm White rayon. Eyes—Dacron georgette. Mouth—Stranded embroidery thread. Hair—Stranded embroidery thread. 210 cm of 3.5 cm lace ribbon. Artificial flower. Petticoat—59 cm by 27.5 cm non-woven fabric. Dress—90 cm by 51 cm lace fabric. 90 cm by 42 cm Pink lining. 130 cm of 3.5 cm lace ribbon. Artificial flower. And Others—No. 18 wire. Packing. Cotton wadding. Polyester batting.

FINISHED SIZE: Refer to diagram.

MAKING INSTRUCTIONS:

Referring to page 50-64 for basic manner, make

hands in same manner as for Stray angels on page 110, make frame as shown on page 132.

Lay wadding on the body in same manner as for Rapunzuel on page 132, sew on bodice with the lining beneath. Sew skirt and its lining respectively, secure to waist 2 pieces together. Decorate neck to front, apply flowers on the skirt.

Pose her with the arm bent, glue sleeve ends together.

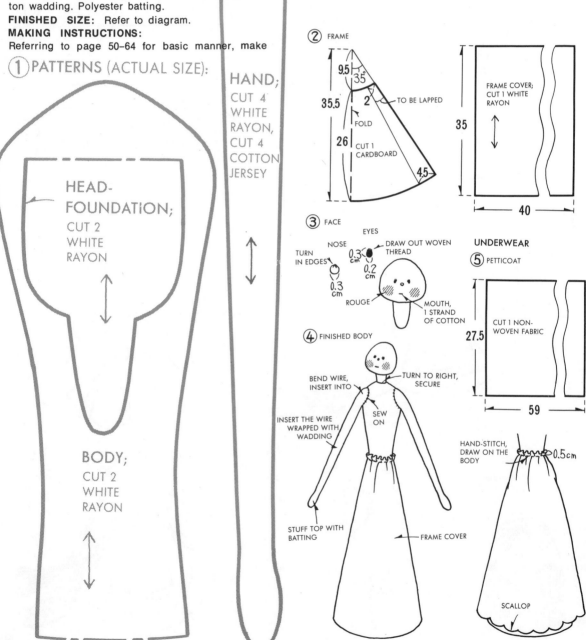

① PATTERNS (ACTUAL SIZE):

HEAD-FOUNDATION; CUT 2 WHITE RAYON

BODY; CUT 2 WHITE RAYON

HAND; CUT 4 WHITE RAYON, CUT 4 COTTON JERSEY

② FRAME

9.5 35°
35.5
2 — TO BE LAPPED
FOLD
26 CUT 1 CARDBOARD
4.5

FRAME COVER; CUT 1 WHITE RAYON
35
40

③ FACE

EYES
NOSE DRAW OUT WOVEN THREAD
TURN IN EDGES 0.3 cm
0.2 cm
0.3 cm
ROUGE
MOUTH, 1 STRAND OF COTTON

④ FINISHED BODY

BEND WIRE, INSERT INTO
TURN TO RIGHT, SECURE
SEW ON
INSERT THE WIRE WRAPPED WITH WADDING
STUFF TOP WITH BATTING
FRAME COVER

UNDERWEAR

⑤ PETTICOAT

CUT 1 NON-WOVEN FABRIC
27.5
59

HAND-STITCH, DRAW ON THE BODY 0.5 cm

SCALLOP

134

DRESS

⑥ CUTTING GUIDE RIGHT SIDE (LACE FABRIC)

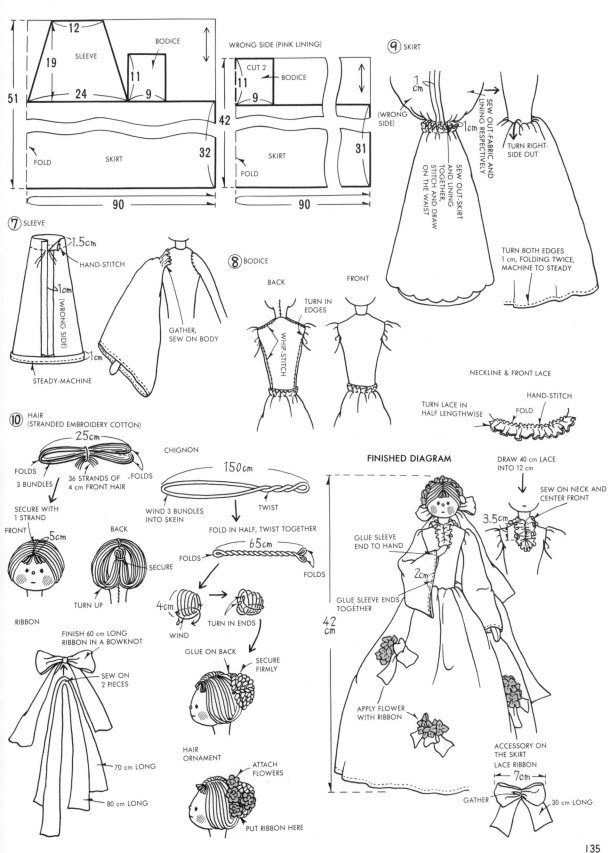

12

SLEEVE

19

24

11

9

BODICE

51

FOLD

SKIRT

32

42

90

WRONG SIDE (PINK LINING)

11

9

CUT 2

BODICE

SKIRT

FOLD

31

90

⑨ SKIRT

1 cm

(WRONG SIDE)

1 cm

SEW OUT-FABRIC AND LINING RESPECTIVELY

SEW OUT-SKIRT AND LINING TOGETHER, STITCH AND DRAW ON THE WAIST

TURN RIGHT-SIDE OUT

TURN BOTH EDGES 1 cm, FOLDING TWICE, MACHINE TO STEADY

⑦ SLEEVE

1.5 cm

HAND-STITCH

1 cm (WRONG SIDE)

1 cm

STEADY-MACHINE

GATHER, SEW ON BODY

⑧ BODICE

BACK

FRONT

TURN IN EDGES

WHIP-STITCH

NECKLINE & FRONT LACE

TURN LACE IN HALF LENGTHWISE

FOLD

HAND-STITCH

DRAW 40 cm LACE INTO 12 cm

SEW ON NECK AND CENTER FRONT

3.5 cm

⑩ HAIR (STRANDED EMBROIDERY COTTON)

25 cm

FOLDS

3 BUNDLES

36 STRANDS OF 4 cm FRONT HAIR

FOLDS

SECURE WITH 1 STRAND

FRONT

5 cm

BACK

SECURE

TURN UP

CHIGNON

150 cm

WIND 3 BUNDLES INTO SKEIN

TWIST

FOLD IN HALF, TWIST TOGETHER

FOLDS

65 cm

FOLDS

4 cm

WIND

TURN IN ENDS

GLUE ON BACK

SECURE FIRMLY

FINISHED DIAGRAM

GLUE SLEEVE END TO HAND

2 cm

GLUE SLEEVE ENDS TOGETHER

42 cm

APPLY FLOWER WITH RIBBON

ACCESSORY ON THE SKIRT LACE RIBBON

7 cm

GATHER

30 cm LONG

RIBBON

FINISH 60 cm LONG RIBBON IN A BOWKNOT

SEW ON 2 PIECES

70 cm LONG

80 cm LONG

HAIR ORNAMENT

ATTACH FLOWERS

PUT RIBBON HERE

ROYAL PRINCESS FROM STARS

Shown on page 40.

If star print fabric is not available, make her the princess of your own choice such as apples, flowers, and birds. Make her face somewhat smaller than its size.

YOU'LL NEED:
Head-Foundation, Body, Hands, Legs—70 cm by 28 cm White rayon. Face, Nose, Hands, Legs—50 cm by 28 cm cotton jersey. Eyes—Dacron georgette. Mouth —Stranded embroidery thread. Hair—Stranded embroidery thread. 13 cm of 2.5 cm broadcloth. Bloomer, Petticoat—88 cm by 27 cm White georgette. Dress, Veil—90 cm by 85 cm dacron print. 72 cm by 37 cm silver lame. 62 cm of 2.5 cm braid. And Others— Packing. Cotton wadding. Polyester batting.
FINISHED SIZE: Refer to diagram.

MAKING INSTRUCTIONS:
Make referring to Hiji on page 50–64 for basic manner.
Stuff polyester batting firmly into hands and legs. Before the bodice is sewn on, lay wadding thinly over the body. Make collar drawing braid, stitch to position.
Put silver lame on wrong side of the veil, steady with slip-stitch.
Sew on hair, put veil over, secure with slip-stitch. Put crown on top.

① PATTERNS (ACTUAL SIZE):

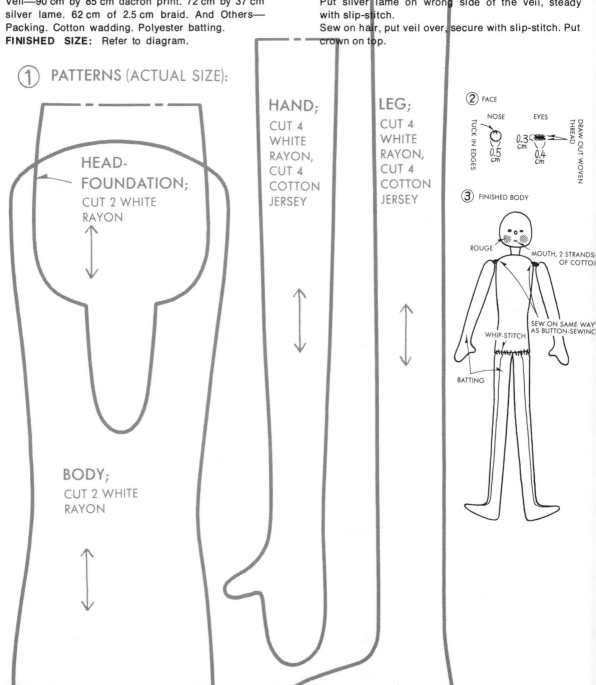

HEAD-FOUNDATION; CUT 2 WHITE RAYON

BODY; CUT 2 WHITE RAYON

HAND; CUT 4 WHITE RAYON, CUT 4 COTTON JERSEY

LEG; CUT 4 WHITE RAYON, CUT 4 COTTON JERSEY

② FACE

TUCK IN EDGES

NOSE
0.5 cm

EYES
0.3 cm
0.4 cm

DRAW OUT WOVEN THREAD

③ FINISHED BODY

ROUGE

MOUTH, 2 STRANDS OF COTTO

SEW ON SAME WAY AS BUTTON-SEWING

WHIP-STITCH

BATTING

DRESS, VEIL, UNDERWEAR

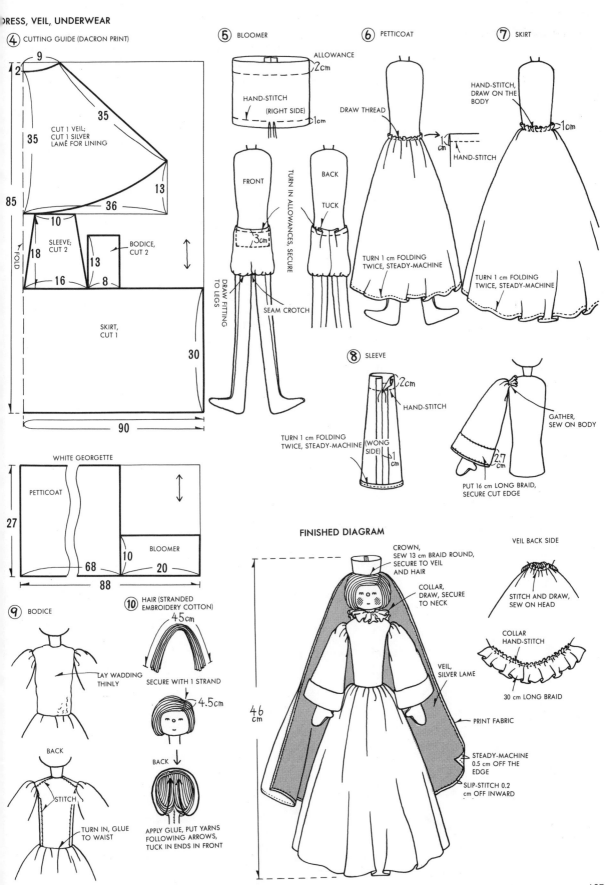

MADAM LILAS

Shown on page 41.

Stuff packing carefully to give a smooth finish to the neck part in front. Pay attention to the level of chignon on back. Finish hair and dress in the shades of lilac.

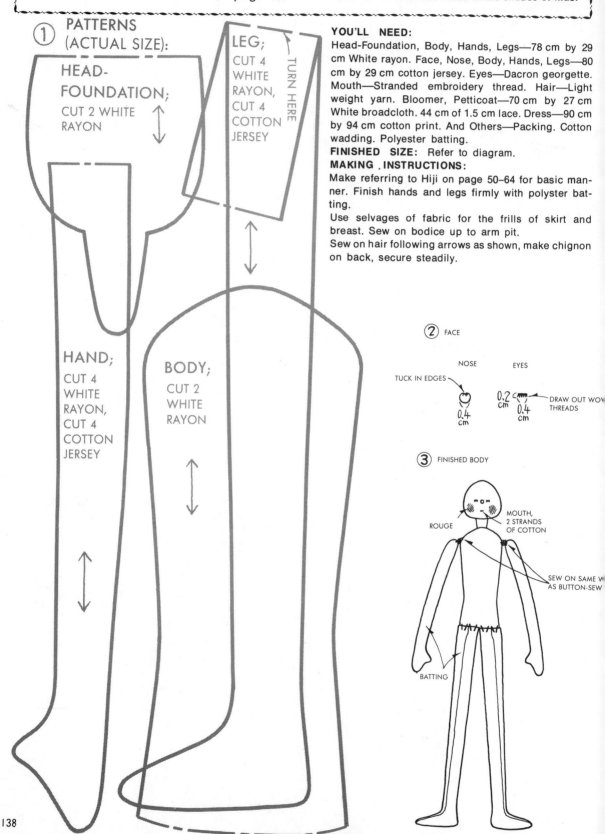

① **PATTERNS (ACTUAL SIZE):**

HEAD-FOUNDATION;
CUT 2 WHITE RAYON

LEG;
CUT 4 WHITE RAYON,
CUT 4 COTTON JERSEY

TURN HERE

HAND;
CUT 4 WHITE RAYON,
CUT 4 COTTON JERSEY

BODY;
CUT 2 WHITE RAYON

YOU'LL NEED:
Head-Foundation, Body, Hands, Legs—78 cm by 29 cm White rayon. Face, Nose, Body, Hands, Legs—80 cm by 29 cm cotton jersey. Eyes—Dacron georgette. Mouth—Stranded embroidery thread. Hair—Light weight yarn. Bloomer, Petticoat—70 cm by 27 cm White broadcloth. 44 cm of 1.5 cm lace. Dress—90 cm by 94 cm cotton print. And Others—Packing. Cotton wadding. Polyester batting.

FINISHED SIZE: Refer to diagram.

MAKING INSTRUCTIONS:
Make referring to Hiji on page 50–64 for basic manner. Finish hands and legs firmly with polyster batting.

Use selvages of fabric for the frills of skirt and breast. Sew on bodice up to arm pit.

Sew on hair following arrows as shown, make chignon on back, secure steadily.

② FACE

NOSE
TUCK IN EDGES
0.4 cm

EYES
0.2 cm
0.4 cm
DRAW OUT WOV THREADS

③ FINISHED BODY

ROUGE
MOUTH, 2 STRANDS OF COTTON
SEW ON SAME V AS BUTTON-SEW
BATTING

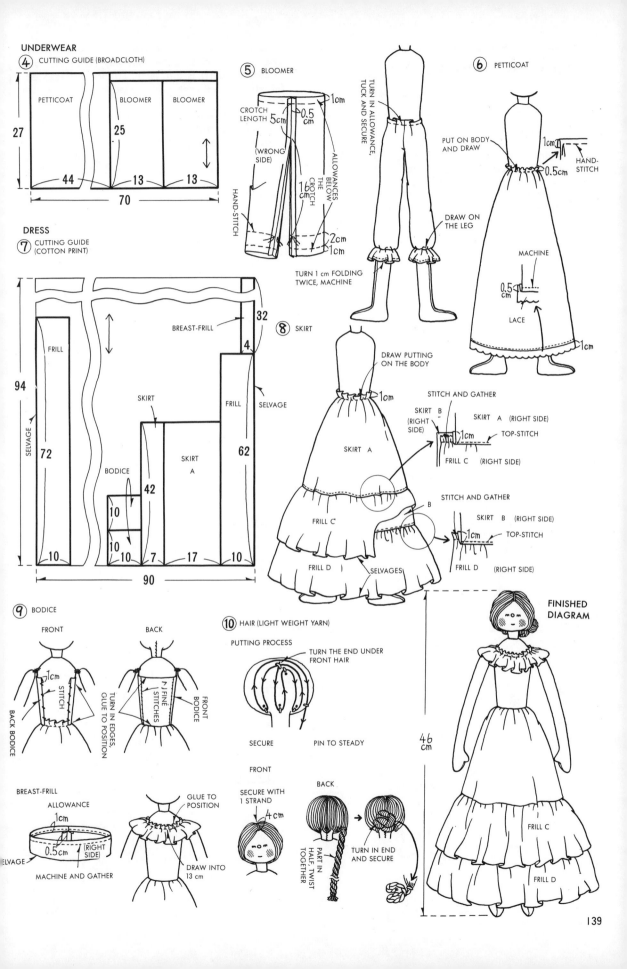

UNDERWEAR

④ CUTTING GUIDE (BROADCLOTH)

PETTICOAT

27

BLOOMER 25

BLOOMER

44   13   13

70

DRESS

⑦ CUTTING GUIDE (COTTON PRINT)

BREAST-FRILL   32

4

FRILL

94

SELVAGE   72   SKIRT   FRILL   62   SELVAGE

BODICE

SKIRT A

42

10

10   10

10   10   7   17   10

90

⑤ BLOOMER

1cm
CROTCH LENGTH   0.5 cm
5cm
(WRONG SIDE)
16cm
ALLOWANCES BELOW THE CROTCH
HAND-STITCH
2cm
1cm
TURN 1cm FOLDING TWICE, MACHINE

TURN IN ALLOWANCE, TUCK AND SECURE

DRAW ON THE LEG

⑥ PETTICOAT

PUT ON BODY AND DRAW
1cm
0.5cm
HAND-STITCH

MACHINE
0.5 cm
LACE
1cm

⑧ SKIRT

DRAW PUTTING ON THE BODY
1cm

SKIRT A

FRILL C

FRILL D   SELVAGES

STITCH AND GATHER
SKIRT B (RIGHT SIDE)   SKIRT A (RIGHT SIDE)
1cm   TOP-STITCH
FRILL C (RIGHT SIDE)

STITCH AND GATHER
B   SKIRT B (RIGHT SIDE)
1cm   TOP-STITCH
FRILL D (RIGHT SIDE)

⑨ BODICE

FRONT   BACK

1cm   STITCH
BACK BODICE
TURN IN EDGES, GLUE TO POSITION
FINE STITCHES
FRONT BODICE

BREAST-FRILL

ALLOWANCE
1cm
0.5cm   (RIGHT SIDE)
SELVAGE
MACHINE AND GATHER

GLUE TO POSITION
DRAW INTO 13 cm

⑩ HAIR (LIGHT WEIGHT YARN)

PUTTING PROCESS
TURN THE END UNDER FRONT HAIR

SECURE   PIN TO STEADY

FRONT
SECURE WITH 1 STRAND
4cm

BACK
PART IN HALF, TWIST TOGETHER
TURN IN END AND SECURE

FINISHED DIAGRAM

46 cm

FRILL C

FRILL D

139

JOHN & BAHBALLA

Shown on page 42.

The twins are made in the same way. Distinguish one is boy, the other is girl, featuring face and legs differently. Make dresses with the fabric of soft in a pale color.

YOU'LL NEED:
Head-Foundation, Body, Hands, Legs—45 cm by 23 cm White rayon. Face, Nose, Hands, Legs—40 cm Beige cotton jersey. Eyes—Dacron georgette. Mouth —Stranded embroidery thread. Hair—Mohair yarn. Dress, Hood, Bloomer—40 cm by 26 cm crepe. 40 cm of 0.6 cm ribbon. 50 cm of 2.5 cm lace. And Others—Packing. Cotton wadding. Polyster batting.

FINISHED SIZE: Refer to diagram.
MAKING INSTRUCTIONS:
Make referring to Hiji shown on page 50–64 for basic manner. Sew on hair, winding yarn round fingers and secure to head all over without snipping the yarn following.

① PATTERNS (ACTUAL SIZE):

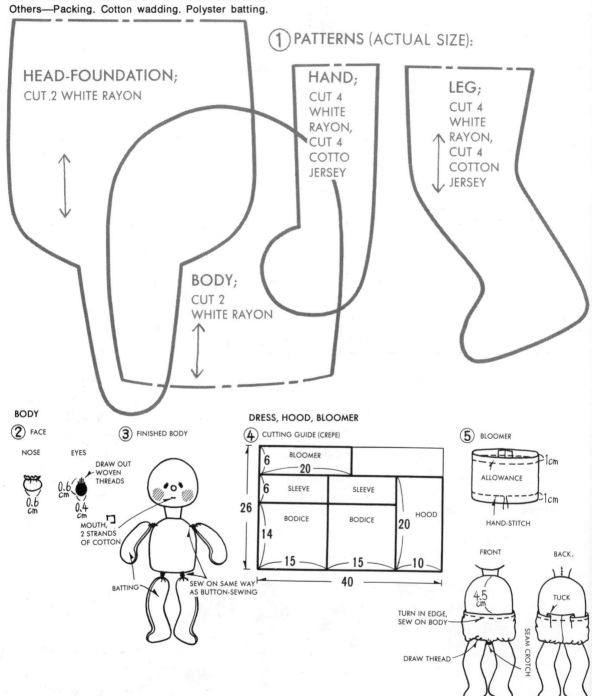

HEAD-FOUNDATION;
CUT 2 WHITE RAYON

HAND;
CUT 4 WHITE RAYON,
CUT 4 COTTO JERSEY

LEG;
CUT 4 WHITE RAYON,
CUT 4 COTTON JERSEY

BODY;
CUT 2 WHITE RAYON

BODY

② FACE

NOSE   EYES

DRAW OUT WOVEN THREADS
0.6 cm
0.4 cm
MOUTH, 2 STRANDS OF COTTON

③ FINISHED BODY

BATTING
SEW ON SAME WAY AS BUTTON-SEWING

DRESS, HOOD, BLOOMER

④ CUTTING GUIDE (CREPE)

6 BLOOMER 20
6 SLEEVE   SLEEVE
26
14 BODICE   BODICE   HOOD 20
15   15   10
40

⑤ BLOOMER

1cm
ALLOWANCE
1cm
HAND-STITCH

FRONT   BACK,

4.5 cm   TUCK

TURN IN EDGE, SEW ON BODY
DRAW THREAD
SEAM CROTCH

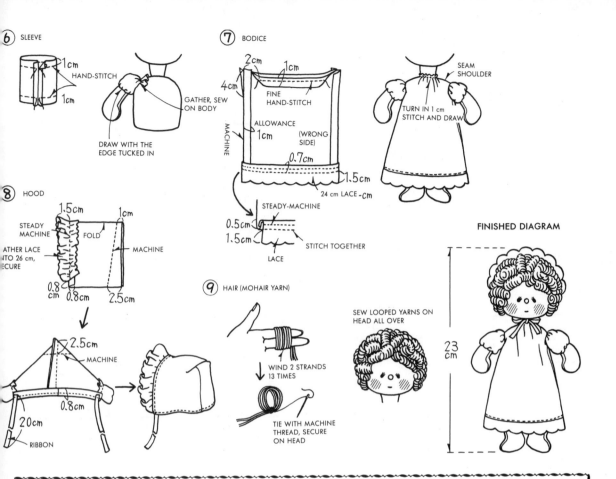

6 SLEEVE

1cm
HAND-STITCH
1cm
DRAW WITH THE EDGE TUCKED IN
GATHER, SEW ON BODY

7 BODICE

2cm
1cm
4cm
FINE HAND-STITCH
MACHINE
ALLOWANCE
1cm
(WRONG SIDE)
0.7cm
1.5cm
24 cm LACE -cm
STEADY-MACHINE
0.5cm
1.5cm
STITCH TOGETHER
LACE

SEAM SHOULDER
TURN IN 1 cm STITCH AND DRAW

8 HOOD

1.5cm
1cm
STEADY MACHINE
FOLD
MACHINE
GATHER LACE INTO 26 cm, SECURE
0.8 cm
0.8cm
2.5cm

2.5cm
MACHINE
0.8cm
20cm
RIBBON

9 HAIR (MOHAIR YARN)

WIND 2 STRANDS 13 TIMES
TIE WITH MACHINE THREAD, SECURE ON HEAD

SEW LOOPED YARNS ON HEAD ALL OVER

FINISHED DIAGRAM

23 cm

MIMI & RULU & POPO

Shown on page 43.

Make the all in same manner. Use an easy-to-handle sheer fabric like lawn. Feature them with their dresses.

YOU'LL NEED (for each):
Head-Foundation, Body, Hands, Legs —40 cm by 27 cm White rayon. Face, Nose, Hands, Legs—50 cm by 15 cm Beige georgette. Eyes—Dacron georgette. Mouth—Stranded embroidery thread. Hair—Frizzle yarn. 20 cm of 0.3 cm ribbon. Bloomer—20 cm by 10 cm White broadcloth. Petticoat—60 cm of 5 cm lace. Dress, Cap—50 cm by 25.5 cm lawn. 28 cm of 1.5 cm lace. And Others—Packing. Cotton wadding. Polyester batting.
FINSIHED SIZE: Refer to diagram.
MAKING INSTRUCTIONS:
Make referring to page 50–64 for basic manner.
Sew on hair in same manner as is shown on page 72.
Make each in same manner and clothe with the dresses various in color.

1 PATTERNS (ACTUAL SIZE):

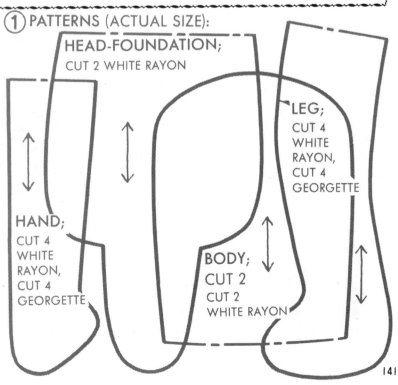

HEAD-FOUNDATION;
CUT 2 WHITE RAYON

LEG;
CUT 4 WHITE RAYON, CUT 4 GEORGETTE

HAND;
CUT 4 WHITE RAYON, CUT 4 GEORGETTE

BODY;
CUT 2
CUT 2 WHITE RAYON

141

② FACE

NOSE
0.4 cm

EYES
0.5 cm
0.3 cm
DRAW OUT WOVEN THREADS

③ FINISHED BODY

ROUGE

MOUTH, 6 STRANDS OF COTTON

SEW ON SAME WAY AS BUTTON-SEWING

BATTING

④ BLOOMER (BROADCLOTH)

CUT 2
10
10

FRONT

5cm

TURN IN 1 cm, SEW ON BODY

BACK

TUCK

DRAW FITTING ON LEGS

ALLOWANCE
1cm

CROTCH LENGTH
3cm

BELOW THE CROTCH
5cm

HAND-STITCH

1cm

⑤ PETTICOAT (LACE)

LAY OVER AND STITCH
5cm
3cm
5cm

30cm

STITCH AND DRAW

0.5cm

DRESS, HOOD

⑥ CUTTING GUIDE

14		BODICE		
5	SLEEVE	8		
5	SLEEVE	8	8	CAP
25.5				8.5	9.5	8.5
11	SKIRT		9	9
	30			
4.5	RIBBON			

50

⑦ SLEEVE

HAND-STITCH
1cm
0.8 cm
1cm

GATHER, SEW ON BODY

DRAW WITH THE EDGE TUCKED IN

⑧ SKIRT

SEW ON BODY
1cm

TURN 1 cm FOLDING TWICE, SLIP-STITCH

⑨ BODICE

FRONT

STITCH SHOULDERS AND SIDES

RIBBON

BACK

FINISH IN BOW KNOT

CUT OFF

TURN 1 cm FOLDING TWICE, MACHINE

FINISHED DIAGRAM

GLUE CAP TO HEAD

25 cm

⑩ HAIR (FRIZZLE YARN)

200 STRANDS OF 32 cm YARN, SECURE IN THE MIDDLE

BRAID 24 STRANDS

16cm

CUT FRONT

RIBBON

⑪ CAP

LACE

1cm
1cm

(WRONG SIDE)

TURN 1 cm FOLDING TWICE, MACHINE

PRINCESS FROM BAMBOO

Shown on page 44.

Those are very simply made. Let them stand putting felt piece over the cardboard. Feature grandparents' faces referring to the picture.

YOU'LL NEED (for each):
Head-Foundation—9 cm by 15 cm White rayon. Face, Nose—20 cm by 20 cm Beige georgette. Eyes—Dacron georgette. Mouth—Stranded embroidery thread. Body—6.5 cm by 13 cm cardboard. And Othe-ers—Packing. Cotton wadding. Polyester batting.
(Princess): Kimono—17 cm by 6.5 cm each, felt Light Pink, Rose. Collar—17 cm by 3 cm each, felt White, Purple. Hair—Sport weight yarn. Ribbon—Stranded cotton small amount each, Yellow Brown, Pnk.
(Grandma): Kimono—6.5 cm by 17 cm felt Dark Blue. Collar—17 cm by 3 cm each, felt White, Grey. Wrin-kles—Silk thread. Hair—Worsted weight yarn.

(Grandpa): kimono—6.5 cm by 17 cm felt Dark Green. Collar—17 cm by 3 cm each, felt White, Brown. Wrinkles—Silk thread. Hair—Worsted weight yarn.
FINISHED SIZE: Refer to diagram.
MAKING INSTRUCTIONS:
Make heads and faces referring to Hiji shown on page 50–64. Finish grandpa's face long lengthwise. Put a little of rounded wadding on the faces of grand-parents right above the mouth. Feature their faces drawing the thread of wrinkles stitched.

① PATTERNS (ACTUAL SIZE):

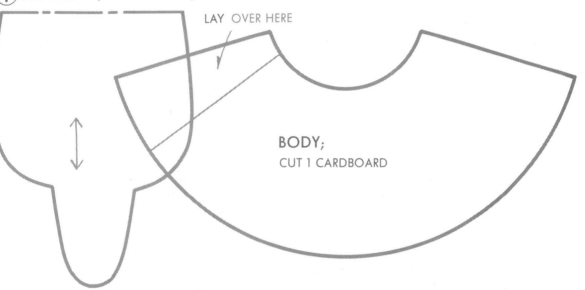

LAY OVER HERE

BODY;
CUT 1 CARDBOARD

KIMONO;
CUT 1 EACH, FELT PINK,
ROSE FOR PRINCESS,
DARK BLUE FOR GRANDMA,
DARK GREEN FOR GRANDPA

CUT 1 EACH, FELT WHITE,
PURPLE FOR PRINCESS,
WHITE, GREY FOR GRANDMA,
DARK GREEN FOR GRANDPA

COLLAR; CUT 1 EACH, FELT
WHITE, PURPLE FOR PRINCESS, WHITE, GREY FOR GRANDMA, DARK GREEN FOR GRANDPA

(PRINCESS)

② FACE

NOSE

0.5 cm

EYES

0.5 cm
0.3 cm

DRAW OUT WOVEN THREADS

③ BODY

GLUE AND STITCH

④ FINISHED BODY

ROUGE

MOUTH, 2 STRANDS OF COTTON

APPLY GLUE ON NECK, INSERT INTO

⑤ KIMONO

COLLAR

WHITE

PURPLE

OVERLAY WHITE, PURPLE IN TURN, GLUE TO STEADY

KIMONO

PINK

ROSE

SECURE INVISIBLY

⑥ HAIR (SPORT YARN)

22cm

200 THREADS

FASTEN

TIE IN THE MIDDLE

APPLY GLUE, ATTACH COMBING NEATLY

TIE 10 STRANDS TOGETHER WITH 6 STRANDS OF EMBROIDERY COTTON YELLOW BROWN, PINK

3cm

FINISHED DIAGRAM

13.5 cm

(GRANDPA, GRANDMA)

① FACE

WRINKLES
SILK 1 STRAND

PUT ROUNDED WADDING, COVER UP WITH SKIN FABRIC

NOSE

0.7 cm

EYES

0.5 cm
0.3 cm

DRAW OUT WOVEN THREADS

ATTACH EYES ON THE WRINKLES

ROUGE

MOUTH, 2 STRANDS OF COTTON

② HAIR (WORSTED YARN)

(GRANDPA)

14cm

TIE 30 STRANDS TOGETHER IN THE MIDDLE, SECURE TO HEAD

SPREAD EVENLY

PASS ROUND SELF-YARN, SECURE WITH MACHINE THREAD

FASTEN WITH THE END TUCKED IN

FASTEN

SEW ON

TIE WITH YARN AND SECURE

BULGE

(GRANDMA)

40 STRANDS OF 32 cm BUNDLE

LAY ACROSS IN THE MIDDLE, SECURE

BACK

GLUE COMBING NEATLY

4.5cm

FASTEN

FINISHED DIAGRAM

(GRANDPA)

15.5 cm

WHITE

BROWN

DARK GREEN

(GRANDMA)

12.5 cm

WHITE

GREY

DARK BLUE

GLOWING SUNSET

Shown on page 45.

Noses are very tiny as you see in the picture. Attach skin fabric cut in nose size to its position. Try to use the fabric of most japaneselike patterns.

YOU'LL NEED (For each):
Head-Foundation—8 cm by 12 cm White rayon. Body, Collar—14 cm by 9 cm cotton fabric. Face, Nose— 10 cm by 10 cm Beige georgette. Eyes—Dacron georgette. Mouth—Stranded embroidery thread. Hair— Sport weight yarn. And Others—Packing. Cotton wadding. Polyester batting.
FINISHED SIZE: Refer to diagram.
MAKING INSTRUCTIONS:
Make referring to page 50–64 for basic manner. Seam body along the pattern, cut out leaving little of allowance all around, turn right side out, stuff packing firmly.

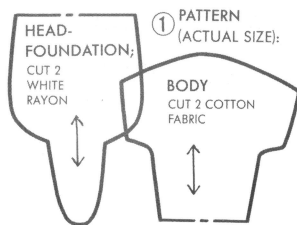

① **PATTERN (ACTUAL SIZE):**

HEAD-FOUNDATION; CUT 2 WHITE RAYON

BODY CUT 2 COTTON FABRIC

② FACE

NOSE

0.3 cm

EYES

DRAW OUT WOVEN THREADS

0.4 cm

0.3 cm

③ BODY

STUFF PACKING

ROUGE

MOUTH, 2 STRANDS OF COTTON

APPLY GLUE ON THE NECK HOLE, INSERT NECK INTO

WHIP-STITCH

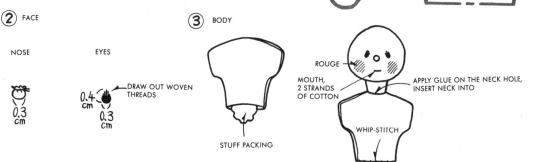

④ COLLAR (COTTON FABRIC)

FOLD HERE

3

9

0.8cm

FRONT

FOLD

GLUE STEADY

SECURE

0.8cm

BACK

GLUE STEADY

SECURE

⑤ HAIR (SPORT YARN)

(GIRL)

14cm

TIE 100 STRANDS TOGETHER

(BOY)

TIE

4 cm YARN 10 STRANDS

10 cm YARN 80 STRANDS

FINISHED DIAGRAMS

(GIRL)

10 cm

, **FINISHED DIAGRAMS**

(BOY)

10.5 cm

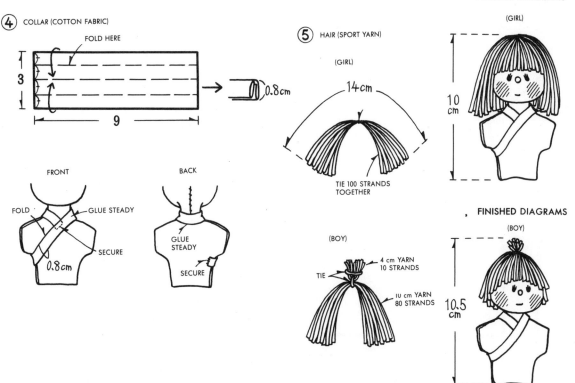

MITCHI

Shown on page 46.

Though she is very tall, the make is simple. Her voluminous skirt is made to keep things inside, so secure its waist firmly to the body.

YOU'LL NEED:
Head-Foundation, Body, Hands—50 cm by 40 cm White rayon. Face, Nose Hands—45 cm by 30 cm cotton jersey. Body—34 cm by 16 cm corduroy. Eyes —Dacron georgette. Mouth—Stranded embroidery thread. Hair—Light weight yarn. Sleeves, Skirt, Hood —90 cm by 80 cm veleveteen. 90 cm of 3 cm lace.

80 cm of 0.7 cm velvet ribbon. In-Pocket—90 cm by 47 cm White rayon. And Others—Packing. Cotton wadding. Polyester batting.
FINISHED SIZE: Refer to diagram.
MAKING INSTRUCTIONS:
Make referring to page 54–64 for basic manner. Machine body corduroy laid over the White rayon.
Sew pocket on the skirt, make a opening center on back.

① PATTERNS (ACTUAL SIZE):

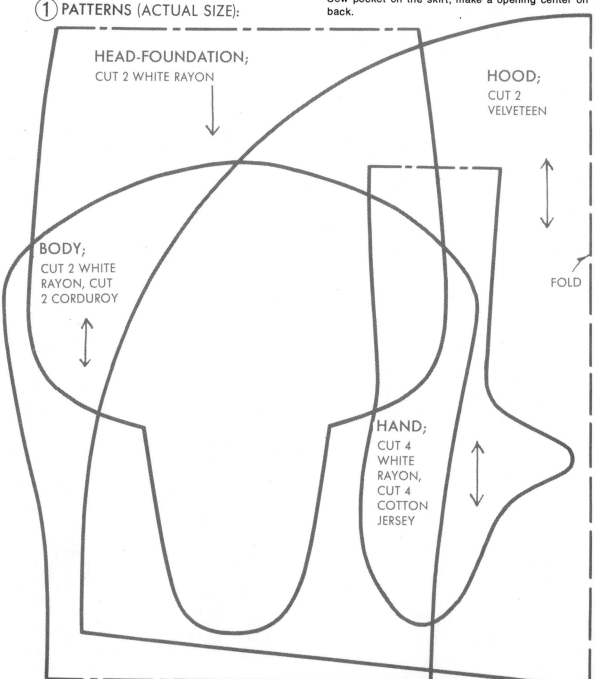

HEAD-FOUNDATION;
CUT 2 WHITE RAYON

HOOD;
CUT 2
VELVETEEN

BODY;
CUT 2 WHITE
RAYON, CUT
2 CORDUROY

FOLD

HAND;
CUT 4
WHITE
RAYON,
CUT 4
COTTON
JERSEY

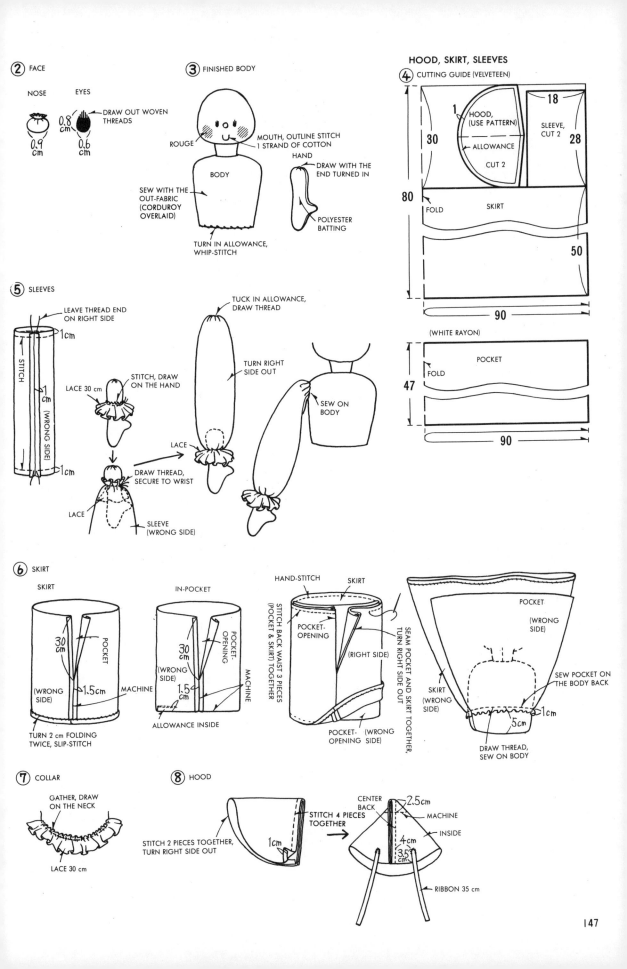

② FACE

NOSE   EYES
→ DRAW OUT WOVEN THREADS
0.8 cm
0.9 cm   0.6 cm

③ FINISHED BODY

ROUGE
MOUTH, OUTLINE STITCH 1 STRAND OF COTTON
HAND
DRAW WITH THE END TURNED IN
BODY
SEW WITH THE OUT-FABRIC (CORDUROY OVERLAID)
POLYESTER BATTING
TURN IN ALLOWANCE, WHIP-STITCH

HOOD, SKIRT, SLEEVES

④ CUTTING GUIDE (VELVETEEN)

30
80
FOLD
1
HOOD, (USE PATTERN)
ALLOWANCE
CUT 2
18
SLEEVE, CUT 2
28
SKIRT
50
90

(WHITE RAYON)
47
FOLD
POCKET
90

⑤ SLEEVES

LEAVE THREAD END ON RIGHT SIDE
1cm
STITCH
1 cm (WRONG SIDE)
1cm
STITCH, DRAW ON THE HAND
LACE 30 cm
DRAW THREAD, SECURE TO WRIST
LACE
SLEEVE (WRONG SIDE)
LACE
TUCK IN ALLOWANCE, DRAW THREAD
TURN RIGHT SIDE OUT
SEW ON BODY

⑥ SKIRT

SKIRT
30 cm
POCKET
(WRONG SIDE)
1.5 cm
MACHINE
TURN 2 cm FOLDING TWICE, SLIP-STITCH

IN-POCKET
POCKET-OPENING
30 cm
(WRONG SIDE)
1.5 cm
MACHINE
ALLOWANCE INSIDE

HAND-STITCH   SKIRT
STITCH BACK WAIST 3 PIECES (POCKET & SKIRT) TOGETHER
POCKET-OPENING
(RIGHT SIDE)
SEAM POCKET AND SKIRT TOGETHER, TURN RIGHT SIDE OUT
POCKET-OPENING (WRONG SIDE)

POCKET
(WRONG SIDE)
SKIRT (WRONG SIDE)
SEW POCKET ON THE BODY BACK
5cm   1cm
DRAW THREAD, SEW ON BODY

⑦ COLLAR

GATHER, DRAW ON THE NECK
LACE 30 cm

⑧ HOOD

STITCH 2 PIECES TOGETHER, TURN RIGHT SIDE OUT
1cm
CENTER BACK
STITCH 4 PIECES TOGETHER
2.5 cm
MACHINE
INSIDE
4 cm
3.5 cm
RIBBON 35 cm

147

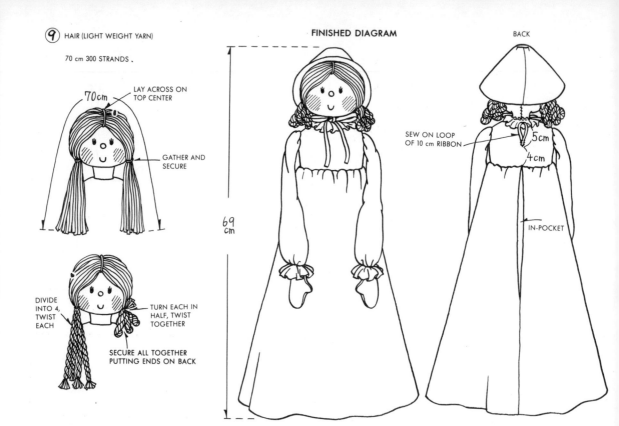

⑨ HAIR (LIGHT WEIGHT YARN)

70 cm 300 STRANDS.

70cm — LAY ACROSS ON TOP CENTER

GATHER AND SECURE

DIVIDE INTO 4, TWIST EACH

TURN EACH IN HALF, TWIST TOGETHER

SECURE ALL TOGETHER PUTTING ENDS ON BACK

FINISHED DIAGRAM

69 cm

BACK

SEW ON LOOP OF 10 cm RIBBON

5cm

4cm

IN-POCKET

ROMMY & DRON

Shown on page 47.

Those are the dolls of long body with short legs. Stuff body carefully to give a smooth finish. Make them marionettes, and enjoy talk manipulating them.

YOU'LL NEED:

(Rommy): Head-Foundation, Hands, Legs—76 cm by 26 cm White rayon. Face, Nose, Hands, Legs—66 cm by 26 cm Beige cotton jersey. Eyes—Dacron georgette. Mouth—Stranded embroidery thread. Hair—Worsted yarn Pink, Blue. No. 30 wire taped Green. Body, Arm, Dress—88 cm by 56 cm velveteen print. 100 cm of 1.5 cm lace. Shoes—36 cm by 16 cm velveteen Navy Blue. 14 cm by 10 cm felt Purple. And Others—Pearl cotton. Packing. Cotton wadding. Polyester batting.

(Dron): Head-Foundation, Hands, Legs—76 cm by 26 cm White Rayon. Face, Nose, Hands—44 cm by 26 cm Beige jersey. Legs—20 cm by 20 cm striped jersey. Eyes—Dacron georgette. Mouth—Stranded embroidery thread. Hair—Worsted yarn Blue, Grey. Body, Arm, Dress—90 cm by 43 cm velveteen Blue Grey. 26 cm of 1.5 cm braid. 22 cm of 2 cm braid. Stranded embroidery cotton. Shoes—36 cm by 16 cm corduroy Brown. 14 cm by 10 cm felt Dark Blue. And Others—Same as Rommy.

MAKING INSTRUCTIONS:

Make referring to page 50–64 for basic manner. Make nose with a scrap of cotton jersey colored in Orange with felt tip pen.

Body and arms are made with dress fabric.

Sew on marionettes' strings of pearl cotton cut in desired length.

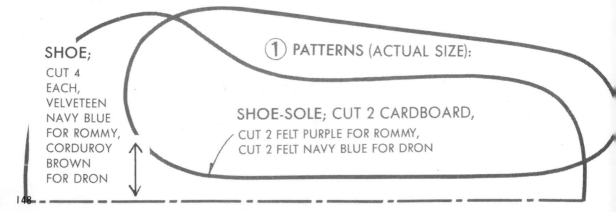

SHOE;

CUT 4 EACH, VELVETEEN NAVY BLUE FOR ROMMY, CORDUROY BROWN FOR DRON

① PATTERNS (ACTUAL SIZE):

SHOE-SOLE; CUT 2 CARDBOARD,
CUT 2 FELT PURPLE FOR ROMMY,
CUT 2 FELT NAVY BLUE FOR DRON

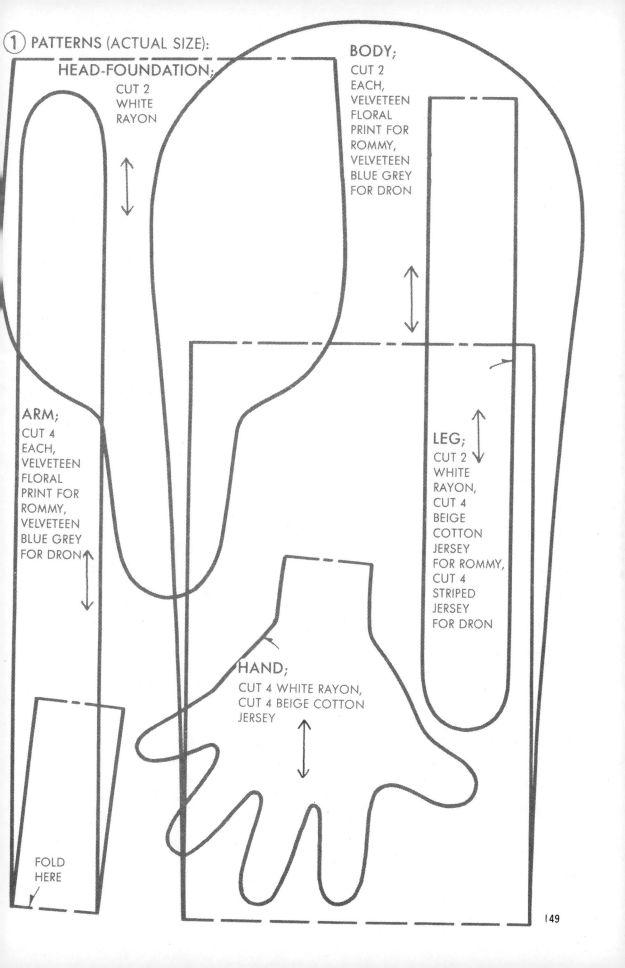

① PATTERNS (ACTUAL SIZE):

HEAD-FOUNDATION;
CUT 2
WHITE
RAYON

BODY;
CUT 2
EACH,
VELVETEEN
FLORAL
PRINT FOR
ROMMY,
VELVETEEN
BLUE GREY
FOR DRON

ARM;
CUT 4
EACH,
VELVETEEN
FLORAL
PRINT FOR
ROMMY,
VELVETEEN
BLUE GREY
FOR DRON

LEG;
CUT 2
WHITE
RAYON,
CUT 4
BEIGE
COTTON
JERSEY
FOR ROMMY,
CUT 4
STRIPED
JERSEY
FOR DRON

HAND;
CUT 4 WHITE RAYON,
CUT 4 BEIGE COTTON
JERSEY

FOLD
HERE

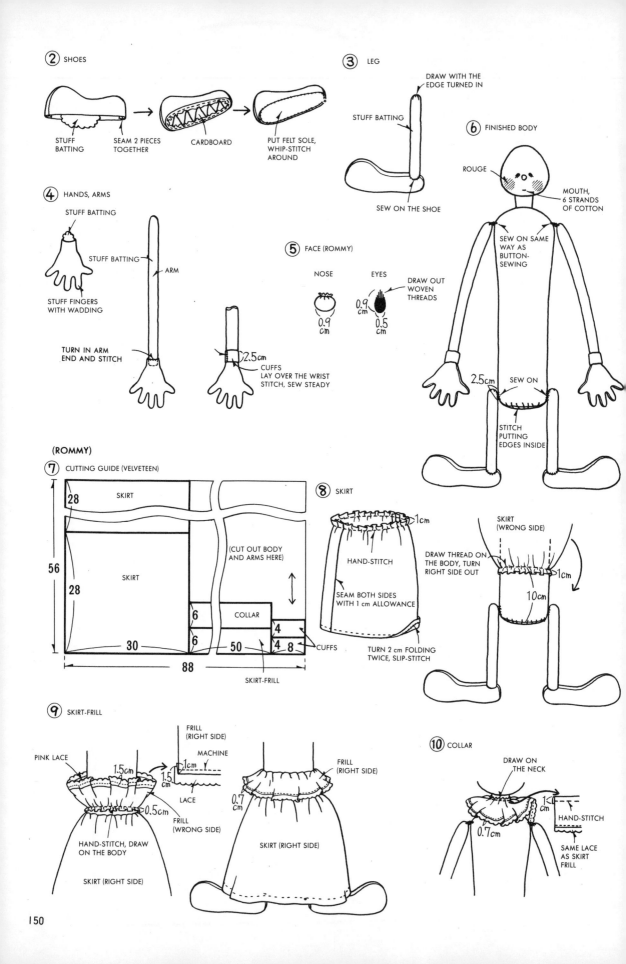

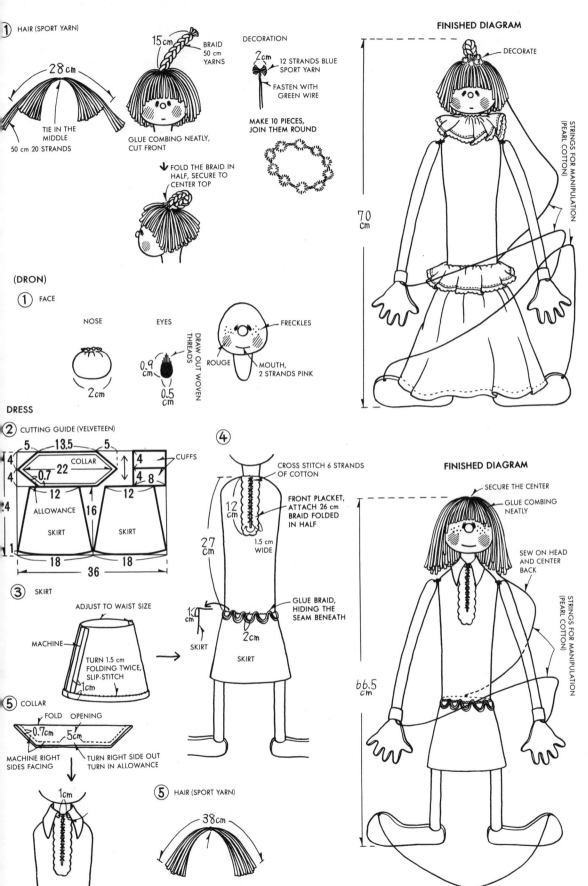

① HAIR (SPORT YARN)

28cm

TIE IN THE MIDDLE
50 cm 20 STRANDS

15cm

BRAID 50 cm YARNS

GLUE COMBING NEATLY, CUT FRONT

↓ FOLD THE BRAID IN HALF, SECURE TO CENTER TOP

DECORATION

2cm

12 STRANDS BLUE SPORT YARN

FASTEN WITH GREEN WIRE

MAKE 10 PIECES, JOIN THEM ROUND

FINISHED DIAGRAM

DECORATE

70 cm

STRINGS FOR MANIPULATION (PEARL COTTON)

(DRON)

① FACE

NOSE

2cm

EYES

0.9 cm

0.5 cm

DRAW OUT WOVEN THREADS

FRECKLES

ROUGE

MOUTH, 2 STRANDS PINK

DRESS

② CUTTING GUIDE (VELVETEEN)

5 13.5 5
4
4 COLLAR 4
   0.7 22 4 8
4 12 12
   ALLOWANCE 16
   SKIRT SKIRT
1
   18 18
       36

CUFFS

③ SKIRT

ADJUST TO WAIST SIZE

MACHINE

TURN 1.5 cm FOLDING TWICE, SLIP-STITCH

1cm

④

CROSS STITCH 6 STRANDS OF COTTON

12 cm

27 cm

1cm

SKIRT

FRONT PLACKET, ATTACH 26 cm BRAID FOLDED IN HALF

1.5 cm WIDE

GLUE BRAID, HIDING THE SEAM BENEATH

2cm

SKIRT

FINISHED DIAGRAM

SECURE THE CENTER

GLUE COMBING NEATLY

SEW ON HEAD AND CENTER BACK

STRINGS FOR MANIPULATION (PEARL COTTON)

66.5 cm

⑤ COLLAR

FOLD OPENING

0.7cm 5cm

MACHINE RIGHT SIDES FACING

TURN RIGHT SIDE OUT TURN IN ALLOWANCE

1cm

⑤ HAIR (SPORT YARN)

38cm

151

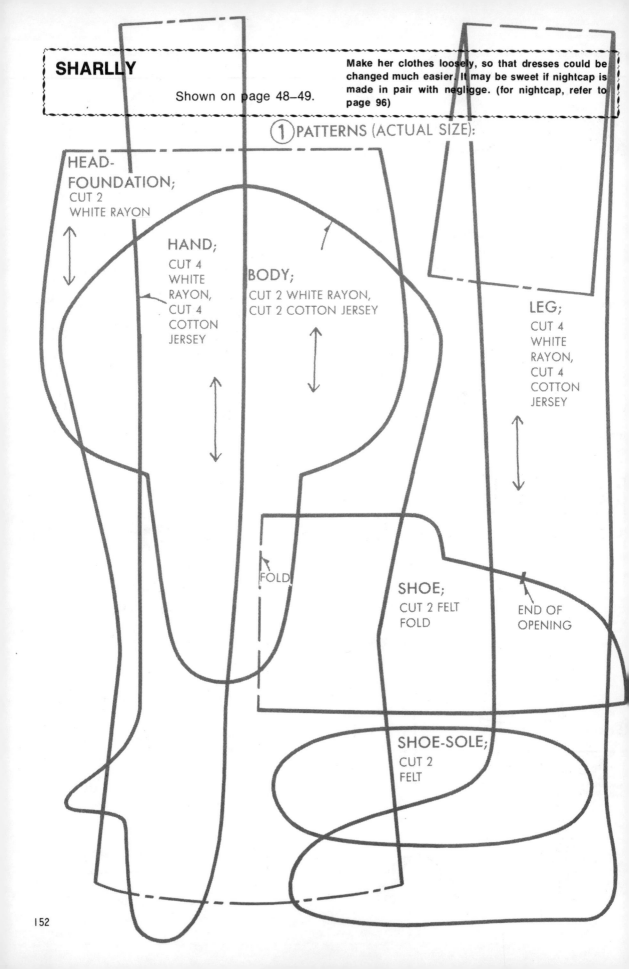

SHARLLY

Shown on page 48–49.

Make her clothes loosely, so that dresses could be changed much easier. It may be sweet if nightcap is made in pair with negligge. (for nightcap, refer to page 96)

①PATTERNS (ACTUAL SIZE):

HEAD-FOUNDATION;
CUT 2
WHITE RAYON

HAND;
CUT 4
WHITE
RAYON,
CUT 4
COTTON
JERSEY

BODY;
CUT 2 WHITE RAYON,
CUT 2 COTTON JERSEY

LEG;
CUT 4
WHITE
RAYON,
CUT 4
COTTON
JERSEY

FOLD

SHOE;
CUT 2 FELT
FOLD

END OF
OPENING

SHOE-SOLE;
CUT 2
FELT

152

YOU'LL NEED:

(Body): Head-Foundation, Body, Hands, Legs—90 cm by 56 cm White rayon. Face, Nose, Body, Hands, Legs—52 cm by 81 cm cotton jersey. Eyes—Dacron georgette. Mouth—Stranded embroidery thread. Hair—Worsted weight yarn.

(Underwear): 70 cm by 40 cm White broadcloth. 80 cm of 2 cm lace. 62 cm of 0.8 cm lace. 2 of 1 cm diamter button. 10 cm of 0.5 cm elastic.

(Blouse): 90 cm by 37 cm crepe. 10 cm by 10 cm floral lace fabric. 3 of 1 cm diamter button. 2 pair of small snaps.

(Jumper-skirt): 85 cm by 32 cm wool. 22 cm of 1.5 cm tyrolean tape. 20 cm long zip fastener.

(Dress): 90 cm by 50 cm cotton print. 10 cm of 2 cm braid. 20 cm long zip fastener.

(Skirt): 62 cm by 40 cm wool print. 40 cm of 0.5 cm elastic.

(Negligge): 55 cm by 125 cm cotton border print. 17 cm of 1.3 cm lace. Elastic thread. 20 cm long zip fastener.

(Hat): Raffia yarn. 100 cm of 3.5 cm lace ribbon. Artificial flower.

(Shoes): 21 cm by 15 cm felt. 40 cm of 0.3 cm ribbon.

FINISHED SIZE: 62 cm tall.

MAKING INSTRUCTIONS:

(Body): Make referring to page 50–64 for basic manner. Sew on hair in same manner as for Cralla shown on page 67. Finish allowances neatly, for seams are visible when clothes are changed.

(Underwear): Sew pants after the lace is sewn on. Fold back allowances of neck and armhols of slip, put lace along, machine steady.

(Blouse): Sew sleeve to side after sleeve top is joined. Sew lace fabric on front.

(Jumper-skirt): Make 7 pin tucks on front. Finish front neck with tyrolean tape.

(Dress): Finish front neck with its facing. Use selvage for hem frill. Pipe sleeve end, sew under arm.

(Skirt): Make 2 rows of casing on the waist, pass elastic through.

(Negligge): Make following border print pattern. Decorate front with shirring and finish with lace stitched on.

(Hat): Work single crochet firmly with size 5/0 croshet hook. Finish with ribbon and flowers.

(Shoes): Join side piece and sole together, using silk thread, pass ribbon through, tie in position.

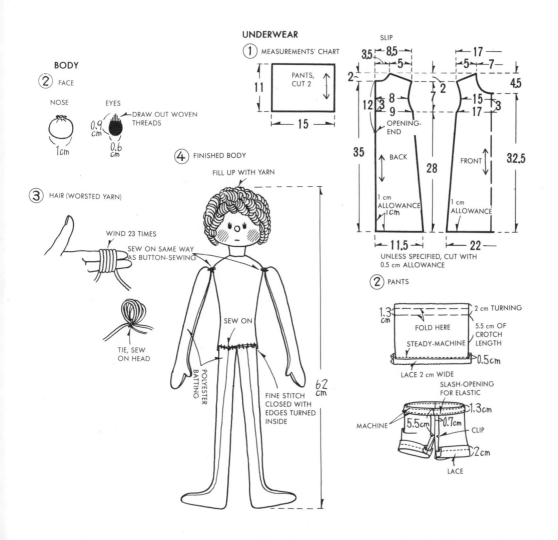

③ SLIP

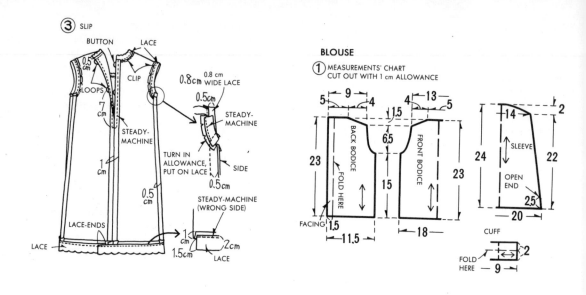

BUTTON
LACE
0.5 cm
LOOPS
7 cm
CLIP
STEADY-MACHINE
1 cm
0.5 cm
LACE-ENDS
LACE
0.8cm WIDE LACE
0.8 cm
0.5cm
STEADY-MACHINE
TURN IN ALLOWANCE, PUT ON LACE
SIDE
0.5cm
STEADY-MACHINE (WRONG SIDE)
1 cm
1.5cm
2cm
LACE

BLOUSE

① MEASUREMENTS' CHART
CUT OUT WITH 1 cm ALLOWANCE

5 9 4 | 4 13 5
1.5
BACK BODICE
FOLD HERE
FACING
23
6.5
15
23
FRONT BODICE
1.5
11.5
18

14 2
SLEEVE
OPEN END
24 22
2.5
20

CUFF
FOLD HERE
9 2

② SEWING

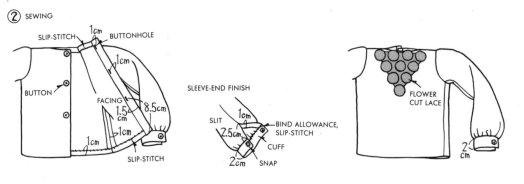

SLIP-STITCH
1cm
BUTTONHOLE
BUTTON
FACING
1cm
1.5 cm
8.5 cm
1cm
1cm
SLIP-STITCH

SLEEVE-END FINISH
SLIT
1cm
2.5cm
2cm
BIND ALLOWANCE, SLIP-STITCH
CUFF
SNAP

FLOWER CUT LACE
2 cm

JUMPER-SKIRT

① MEASUREMENTS' CHART

3.5
BACK BODICE CUT 2
DART
10
5
5
2.5 7 1.5
4

2.5 cm FOR PIN-TUCKS INCLUDED
3.5 8 3.5
FRONT BODICE
6 5
6
5
15
0.5 cm ALLOWANCE

12
10
BACK SKIRT, CUT 2
END OF OPENING
29
15
2 cm ALLOWANCE

25
FRONT SKIRT
29
31

UNLESS SPECIFIED, CUT WITH 1 cm ALLOWANCE

② SEWING

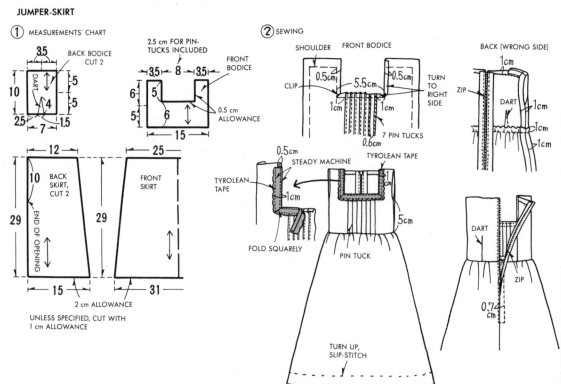

SHOULDER FRONT BODICE
CLIP
0.5cm
5.5 cm
0.5cm
TURN TO RIGHT SIDE
1cm
1cm
7 PIN TUCKS
0.6cm

BACK (WRONG SIDE)
1cm
ZIP
DART
1cm
1cm
1cm

0.5cm
STEADY MACHINE
TYROLEAN TAPE
TYROLEAN TAPE
1cm
5cm
FOLD SQUARELY
PIN TUCK

DART
ZIP
0.74 cm

TURN UP, SLIP-STITCH

DRESS

① MEASUREMENTS' CHART

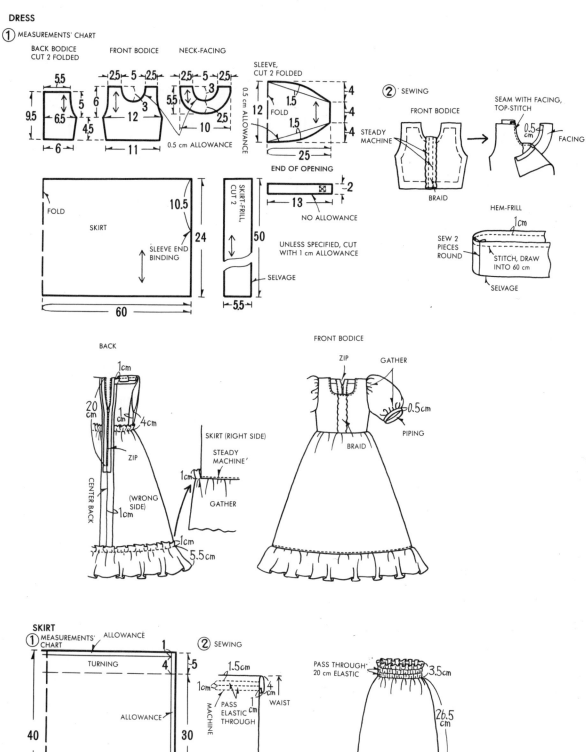

BACK BODICE CUT 2 FOLDED

FRONT BODICE

NECK-FACING

5.5

9.5 — 5 — 6.5

6 — 4.5

6

SLEEVE, CUT 2 FOLDED

2.5 — 5 — 2.5 — 3

6 — 12 — 3

11

2.5 — 5 — 2.5 — 3

5.5 — 1 — 2.5

10

0.5 cm ALLOWANCE

0.5 cm ALLOWANCE

12 FOLD

1.5

1.5

25

4 — 4 — 4

② SEWING

FRONT BODICE

SEAM WITH FACING, TOP-STITCH

STEADY MACHINE

BRAID

0.5 cm

FACING

END OF OPENING

13 — 2

NO ALLOWANCE

UNLESS SPECIFIED, CUT WITH 1 cm ALLOWANCE

FOLD

SKIRT

10.5

24

SLEEVE END BINDING

60

SKIRT-FRILL, CUT 2

50

5.5

SELVAGE

HEM-FRILL

1cm

SEW 2 PIECES ROUND

STITCH, DRAW INTO 60 cm

SELVAGE

BACK

1cm

20 cm

1 cm — 4cm

ZIP

CENTER BACK

(WRONG SIDE)

1cm

1cm

5.5cm

SKIRT (RIGHT SIDE)

STEADY MACHINE

1cm

GATHER

FRONT BODICE

ZIP

GATHER

0.5 cm

PIPING

BRAID

SKIRT

① MEASUREMENTS' CHART

ALLOWANCE

1 — 4 — 5

TURNING

ALLOWANCE

40

30

TURNING

62 — 5

1

② SEWING

1.5 cm

1cm

MACHINE

PASS ELASTIC THROUGH

4 cm — 1

WAIST

HEM

cm — 4 cm

SLIP-STITCH

PASS THROUGH 20 cm ELASTIC

3.5cm

26.5 cm

155

NEGLIGGE

UNLESS SPECIFIED, CUT WITH 1 cm ALLOWANCE

SHIRR INTO PARENTHESIZED MEASURE

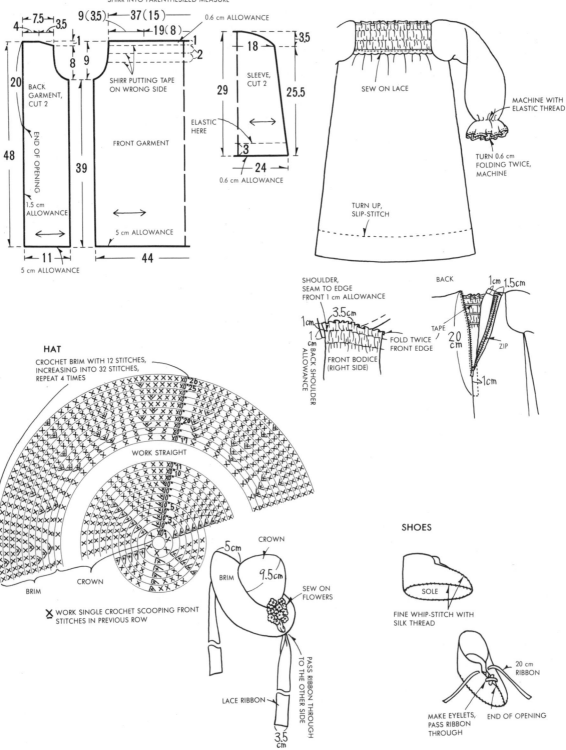

BACK GARMENT, CUT 2

END OF OPENING

1.5 cm ALLOWANCE

5 cm ALLOWANCE

FRONT GARMENT

SHIRR PUTTING TAPE ON WRONG SIDE

ELASTIC HERE

5 cm ALLOWANCE

0.6 cm ALLOWANCE

SLEEVE, CUT 2

0.6 cm ALLOWANCE

SEW ON LACE

TURN UP, SLIP-STITCH

MACHINE WITH ELASTIC THREAD

TURN 0.6 cm FOLDING TWICE, MACHINE

SHOULDER, SEAM TO EDGE FRONT 1 cm ALLOWANCE

BACK SHOULDER ALLOWANCE

FRONT BODICE (RIGHT SIDE)

FOLD TWICE FRONT EDGE

BACK

TAPE

ZIP

HAT

CROCHET BRIM WITH 12 STITCHES, INCREASING INTO 32 STITCHES, REPEAT 4 TIMES

WORK STRAIGHT

BRIM

CROWN

X WORK SINGLE CROCHET SCOOPING FRONT STITCHES IN PREVIOUS ROW

CROWN

BRIM

SEW ON FLOWERS

LACE RIBBON

PASS RIBBON THROUGH TO THE OTHER SIDE

SHOES

SOLE

FINE WHIP-STITCH WITH SILK THREAD

MAKE EYELETS, PASS RIBBON THROUGH

END OF OPENING

20 cm RIBBON